RUNNING THE AMERICAN CORPORATION

 The American Assembly, *Columbia University*

RUNNING
THE
AMERICAN
CORPORATION

Prentice-Hall, Inc., *Englewood Cliffs, New Jersey*

A SPECTRUM BOOK

Library of Congress Cataloging in Publication Data
Main entry under title:

Running the American corporation.

(The American Assembly series) (A Spectrum Book)
At head of title: The American Assembly, Columbia University.
"This book, organized and edited by Dean William R.
Dill . . . was first read in draft by the participants in
the Fifty-fourth American Assembly, Arden House,
Harriman, New York, April 1978."
Includes index.
1. Corporations—United States—Addresses, essays,
lectures. 2. Industry—Social aspects—United States—
Addresses, essays, lectures. 3. Industrial management
—United States—Addresses, essays, lectures. I. Dill,
William R. II. American Assembly.
HD2741.R84   658.4′08   78-16922
ISBN 0-13-783894-8
ISBN 0-13-783886-7 pbk.

10 9 8 7 6 5 4 3 2 1

PRENTICE-HALL INTERNATIONAL, INC. (*London*)
PRENTICE-HALL OF AUSTRALIA PTY, LTD. (*Sydney*)
PRENTICE-HALL OF CANADA, LTD. (*Toronto*)
PRENTICE-HALL OF INDIA PRIVATE LIMITED (*New Delhi*)
PRENTICE-HALL OF JAPAN, INC. (*Tokyo*)
PRENTICE-HALL OF SOUTHEAST ASIA PTE., LTD. (*Singapore*)
WHITEHALL BOOKS LIMITED (*Wellington, New Zealand*)

Table of Contents

Preface

Corporate Governance. In the words of a prominent journalist, it is a "fancy term for the various influences that determine what a corporation does and does not do or should and should not do." Fancy term or not, it finds recognition and understanding in virtually every executive office and boardroom in the nation. We ourselves would add that governance relates to corporate response to the needs and expectations of shareholders and other claimants, such as consumers, employees, and the community; it refers to *Running the American Corporation* vis-à-vis many new pressures for change. It is also an expression, especially in government circles, of what a corporation may or may not do.

The issue of governance is therefore a timely one. In one rubric it fixes on a number of questions asked by many constituents of the corporation. Questions about profitability, efficiency, productivity, and long-term economic prospects. Questions about employment policies, overseas operations, environmental decisions, quality of products. Questions about whether the corporation should help solve the staggering national problems that go beyond its own economic scope, whether indeed the corporation is *able* to do so. Questions about the sheer size and power of corporations and whether the tradition of self-regulation, which has deep roots in our society, is a strong enough bulwark against portents of other regulation: questions asked by government. And so on.

This book, organized and edited by Dean William R. Dill of the New York University Graduate School of Business, was first read in draft by the participants in the Fifty-fourth American Assembly, Arden House, Harriman, New York, April 1978, as background for their deliberations. (The report of that meeting, "Corporate Governance in America," may be had from The American Assembly.) But it is intended also for, indeed especially for, all who are exposed in one way or another to the influence of the American corporation —in other words, most of us.

The opinions herein do not belong to the nonpartisan, public affairs forum The American Assembly any more than to The Ford Foundation or the individuals and corporations who helped underwrite the project. The authors are on their own, but we are pleased to present their analyses and ideas for public consideration.

Clifford C. Nelson
President
The American Assembly

William R. Dill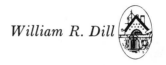

Introduction

Since the days of Henry Ford and Frederick W. Taylor, the most important initiatives to improve the running of American corporations have come under the rubric of *management.* New conceptual tools improved the ability of companies to marshal and use resources efficiently, to motivate human effort, and to control performance over an increasingly complex variety of production and marketing tasks. Companies learned to think and plan strategically about directions in which they should develop and then to organize systematically for innovation and change. New technologies—ranging from the telephone and computer systems to satellite communications and jet aircraft—extended the intellectual and organizational powers of managers and increased their mobility for overseeing diversified, far-flung operations. Financial, organizational, and technological approaches tested in business proved useful for strengthening the management of other social institutions, from hospitals and universities to the defense establishment.

It was not unreasonable for Peter Drucker to describe business management as "the success story of this century." According to his book called *Management,* these achievements enable

> . . . us today to promise—perhaps prematurely (and certainly rashly) — the abolition of the grinding poverty that has been mankind's lot through the ages. It is largely the achievement of business management that advanced societies today can afford mass higher education. That we today consider it . . . an imperfection of society for people to be fixed in their opportunities and jobs by class and birth . . . is a result of our economic performance, that is, of the performance of business management. In a world that is politically increasingly fragmented and

obsessed by nationalism, business management is one of the very few institutions capable of transcending national boundaries.

It is also business management to which our society increasingly looks for leadership in respect to the quality of life. Indeed, what sounds like harsh criticism of business management tends often to be the result of high, perhaps unrealistically high, expectations based on the past performance. . . . "If you can do so well, why don't you do better?"

The men running American corporations have managed not only to make them big, powerful, and profitable, but also have striven to make them efficient and responsive to changing societal demands and preferences—even to the point of realizing that by the time this century ends and the next begins, that "the men running . . ." should have become "the men and women running American corporations."

Yet management today finds its successes tarnished by accusations of failure, its contributions overshadowed by charges of malfeasance, its autonomy threatened by new proposals for oversight and control. Some of this disappointment results from corporations failing to fulfill their basic production, marketing, and profit-seeking tasks well. Some relates to abuse of corporate powers and to renewed controversy about the adequacy of ground rules under which corporations have been designed to operate: the drive for short-term earnings versus goals for long-term improvement of quality of life in society and the competitive pursuit of personal gain versus reasonable standards of morality and service to fellow man. Much relates to a basic unease about "who governs?" Company executives often seem insulated from effective control by directors and shareholders, to whom they are legally responsible, and still more from control by others such as customers, employees, and community groups who have a stake in how corporations perform.

Even such a defender of business and of management as Peter Drucker acknowledges that troubled times lie ahead. The manager who wants to keep his business autonomous, according to Drucker, must recognize that he is a public man, serving public needs. His earnings and his job security should depend squarely on what he accomplishes for society. The base for corporate legitimacy and for his authority is not the pursuit of profits for shareholders, but the ability "to make human strength productive" for the entire community.

Thus the theme of this book about running the American corporation is not management, but *governance*. How do business and society work together to decide the limits within which corporate managers may exercise initiative? What are reasonable rules of the game, and how should they be enforced? How should rules be modified to fit shifting circumstances (like the growing importance of multinational corporations) or constrained to accommodate special social goals (such as increased job opportunities for minorities)? With respect to the many different and competing claimants—investors, employees, customers, suppliers, neighbors, victims of pollution, etc.—for influence and service, how is the large public corporation to be held accountable? Should accountability remain—as it is largely now—giving people a chance to judge performance and results after the fact, or should it include seeking ways to give citizens whose lives are affected by corporations a larger voice in corporate planning for the future? Can we guide managerial behavior to satisfy aspirations that corporations be not only prosperous, but moral; not only efficient, but attentive to aesthetic and spiritual values; not only supportive of freedom for the enterprise, but protective of freedom for individuals?

Governance for the authors represented here is not simply another word for government regulation and control. The concept embraces ideas for possible new legislation: i.e., changes in disclosure and reporting requirements, federal rather than state chartering of corporations, laws sharpening the liabilities of auditors and directors, or the addition of a consumer protection agency to groups already set up to oversee business actions on occupational health and safety, pensions, product quality, energy use, and pollution control. But the concept also covers many steps that can be taken—and may better be taken—without legislation: changes in the composition and duties of boards of directors, improvements to corporate planning systems, and new incentives and controls that will keep managers and professionals at all levels within a firm in better tune with what society expects. While many discussions of governance concentrate primarily on legal solutions, we have tried to reflect on what both law and management can accomplish.

The trick in reforming business is to avoid doing more harm than good; thus, we have been cautious about proposals for sweeping solutions. We do not want to make corporations less diverse, less creative, or less productive. Nor by delegating some of the new oversight responsibilities to government do we want to risk building unresponsive concentrations of power there at the cost of freedoms for both business and individual citizens. For some reforms, legislative mandates will be best. For others, voluntary action should suffice. And in between, much improvement in governance may result simply from opening new kinds of direct dialogue between corporate leaders and their many constituencies. A better marketplace of advice, preferences, and pressures—to supplement customers' decisions on products or shareholders' decisions on investments—may ultimately be the best way to keep corporations and society together.

Our discussion of the governance problem begins by examining its origins. The chapter which follows this introduction reviews the evolution of corporations as economic and social institutions in the United States and highlights the questions of performance, power, and managerial professionalism that have moved the question of governance to center stage. In Chapter 2, Lewis Young charts the many claimants for influence over the corporation. He examines how the interests and aspirations of traditional constituencies like shareholders and consumers have changed and how new constituencies like environmentalists have emerged to seek influence over corporate decisions.

Chapters 3 and 4 look at mechanisms for influence from outside the corporation. Elliott Weiss discusses the organizational and legal systems which have evolved to give shareholders an effective voice in what companies do. He asks how well the electoral process, the proxy process, and opportunities for legal challenge and redress have served investors and how well rules and practices for disclosure of information about corporate actions and results have reinforced shareholder powers. Weiss presents ideas to strengthen the shareholders' role in governance, and evaluates the degree to which mechanisms designed for shareholders are relevant to meeting the needs of other, newer claimants.

Laurence Moss uses the example of trying to influence corporate behavior on environmental issues to examine the problems—with new kinds of constituencies and in the heat of controversy—of developing new approaches to governance. He compares the advantages of legislative and regulatory actions by government to the advantages of nongovernmental negotiations and accommodations, and he talks about the part that private interest groups like environmental study or action coalitions can play as intermediaries for business, government, and the public.

Reginald Jones and Lee Seidler deal with two groups that have been judged to have pivotal responsibilities for insuring that management performs well and behaves ethically for both shareholders and society. Jones examines the corporate board of directors, the ways in which their composition and duties have been changing, and the strengths and weaknesses of various proposals for making boards more effective. Seidler discusses the independent auditor and the standard-setting groups within the accounting profession who, with the Securities and Exchange Commission, set the rules by which corporate financial performance will be measured. Both chapters assume that changes are desirable, but both raise fundamental questions about relative roles of the private sector and of government in setting the direction and the pace for change.

The last two chapters bring us back from governance to management. No reforms from outside will be effective unless there are also changes in the way that managers do their job within the firm. John deButts works from his perspective as chief executive of American Telephone and Telegraph to describe how managers can build the demands and preferences of society into the corporate strategic plan. Much of the argument about governance comes down to disagreement about the way management sets goals, makes investments, and orchestrates company operations. Thus, if plans anticipate better what various constituencies will expect in judging ultimate performance, pressures for other kinds of reform may diminish.

Melvin Anshen discusses more broadly the challenges that questions about governance pose to management structure and functioning, from top to lowest levels within the corporation. He samples the impact of changing expectations on many groups within the managerial hierarchy. He explores not only questions about changes in duties and responsibilities, but implications for incentive and control structures and for management selection and development.

Of necessity, within the limits of a small book, we have dealt with governance questions mainly as we see them in the United States. We have ventured some comparisons to governance issues as they have emerged in Europe and other parts of the world. Much more emphasis overseas has been on the role of employees and trade unions in running the corporation. Consumer and environmental pressures in other countries have varied in degree and emphasis. Issues like payments to sales agents and bribes to government officials, which have produced cries for reform in American corporations, have created relatively little stir for foreign multinationals.

As you sample the viewpoints in our chapters and add to them by other reading and discussion, it is important to think about international dimensions of the governance issue. Large public American corporations are almost inevitably today multinational corporations; and many large foreign corporations are important participants in the American economy and society. The solutions we choose to make corporations run better must, first and foremost, fit American needs and traditions. Increasingly, though, they will have to be weighed against overseas conditions as well.

Finally, this book follows an earlier American Assembly volume, *The Ethics of Corporate Conduct.* Many people who want to achieve improvements in corporate morality believe that the route lies through changes in corporate governance. Such changes can help, but changes in structure alone will not work unless society is also clear about the goals and standards which structure is intended to help achieve. Setting such goals and standards for business and society today is more complex than ever. Improvements in governance can help corporations make better choices about how to behave and about the ways in which they try to serve. But whatever the governance structure, where individuals and groups in society are not in agreement about what they expect from business, corporate executives will continue to mirror that conflict in their decisions and actions.

William R. Dill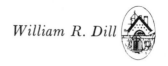

1

Private Power
and Public Responsibility

Any discussion of corporate governance—of reform in the way that large companies and society manage their relationships with one another—should start from three premises. First is that the present system and institutions of business have done extremely well for most of us as individuals, as a nation, and as members of a world community. It is difficult to find an alternative approach to economic and managerial organization that has been half as effective. Planners in eastern Europe are borrowing much more heavily these days from General Electric than from Karl Marx to improve productivity and social responsiveness in their state-owned, bureaucratically-run industrial enterprises.

Second is that public confidence and trust in business have declined. The problems which have accompanied business success, and which often have been side-consequences of that success, are serious ones for society. They cannot be brushed away by corporate leaders. In many instances society is growing impatient because the prob-

WILLIAM R. DILL *is Dean of the Faculty of Business Administration and Professor of Management at New York University. Formerly with IBM Corporation, he is director of four companies, Chairman of the Board of Judges of* Financial World's *annual report competition, chairman of the New York Metropolitan Advertising Review Board, and author of numerous books and articles on management.*

lems are not new and because both effort and progress toward
change seem weak.

Compare your favorite list of questions or complaints about corporations, for example, to the reforms that John Maurice Clark
thought important in 1925 when he published *Social Control of
Business.* He wanted companies to do a better job of producing
efficiently, satisfying customers, and earning returns on capital. He
thought they should help stabilize the world political situation and
provide "international security against war." He cited problems of

> industrial safety and health, representation of laborers and consumers in
> industry, wages and other incentives, the adjustment of labor disputes,
> the effects of industry on labor, efficiency and waste, conservation, the
> relation of industry to regional and city planning, the problems of
> agriculture and coal mining, and the wastes of advertising and sales-
> manship.

Clark continued:

> Most fundamental is the question of the needs of human beings, as
> workers and consumers, . . . both quantitative needs for economic
> goods and qualitative needs for desirable conditions of life and of social
> and moral relations to one's fellows, which are decidedly dependent on
> the organization of industry.

The third premise is that we do not have what can fairly be called
a "crisis" in corporate governance. Whatever the level of criticism
today, some historians argue that it is far less than business faced in
the 1890s or in the early 1920s. We do have—after an unusual period
of prosperity and public confidence in business that followed World
War II—the serious resumption of some old debates.

One side in these debates warns us that we must not casually
abandon the basic design principles from which modern corporations grew. For more than 200 years we have encouraged private
initiative and competition for profits in business, not because this
was the noblest concept of how individuals could be motivated or
how a society might run, but because it promised to be the most
effective way to get individuals to work hard and to take large risks
in order to satisfy society's needs. We granted priority of rights to
owners of a business because they would absorb risk and because
drives for self-aggrandizement could be channeled into actions that
would serve customers and employees as well. We endorsed aggressive growth and development because we wanted it as a society. We
agreed that marketplace decisions between buyer and seller should

dominate as a source of direction and discipline because we wanted end users to judge results and we wanted firms to be able to fail. Whatever the transitional costs of failure, it seemed better when a business was not meeting a market need, for capital and human resources to be released for reallocation to other ventures.

Although one of the real issues about the modern corporation is the size and power that many have attained, our general approach to regulating and controlling concentrations of power has not been to install another authority center over them in hierarchical fashion, as happens under state socialism. It has been to respond by efforts to check and counterbalance the power, either through mechanisms like antitrust which try to disperse it again or by encouragement of the growth of centers of countervailing influence, such as labor unions, the press, and environmental groups in the private sector or regulatory agencies of federal and local governments. As a society, we have an affinity for competitive and adversarial approaches and an aversion, outside the corporation itself, to integrated planning and centralized management.

Even sharp critics of many corporate actions support private enterprise and initiative in the economic sphere and worry about restricting the liberty of corporations in defining and pursuing market-determined goals. Market freedom and political freedom have been related rallying cries through most of American history, even though a careful examination of the evidence suggests that the two may not be as completely interdependent as many businessmen would like us to believe.

The other side in the debates reminds us that nothing which has gone before or that exists today was ordained by the Almighty. From debates in the eighteenth century about how to cure the abuses of mercantilism and autocratic governments, Adam Smith and his followers laid out a design which formed the basis for our present economic system; and the founding fathers of the American Republic started the modern world's first major experiment in political democracy. Their prescriptions are now frequently quoted as holy writ, even though Adam Smith had little regard for the corporation as a form of economic organization, and George Washington had no inkling of the kinds of governmental structures that have accumulated by popular will today. To each man, General Motors and the Federal Trade Commission might both be frightening to contemplate!

Yesterday's ideology gives the corporation no fundamental protection against more radical demands for change. The corporation exists, with a license to emphasize profit seeking and economic measures of performance and with a right to lecture society about the limits of its noneconomic responsibilities, only as long as society believes such structures and such limits on goals and performance serve its overall needs. Chester Barnard, a former executive in the AT&T system, stressed the stark fundamentals in *The Functions of the Executive*. To Barnard a corporation—and any other organization—exists to take resources or "contributions" from some parties (money from investors and customers, materials from suppliers, energy and talent from employees, grants of freedom to operate from government, etc.) and to convert these contributions into services or "inducements" for the same parties and others (dividends and interest back to investors, goods or services to customers, payments to suppliers and employees, actions producing welfare for the surrounding community, etc.). No participant in the process (like shareholders) has a priority claim unless other participants grant it as a way to improve their own return. For Barnard the organizational calculus was simple: to the extent that the inflow of contributions and the effectiveness of the conversion process more than cover the demands for inducements and services in return, a corporation will flourish and grow. To the extent that what a corporation can generate as inducements does not sustain the flow of contributions it needs, it will decline and eventually fail.

His paradigm is simple and abstract, but it carries an essential truth. Corporations have been allowed by society to play by a special set of rules. Yet these rules, by which most would like to continue to play, will only stay in force if society believes that corporate structures and competitive markets are better than other approaches for creating, producing, and distributing the goods and services they desire. The ultimate bottom line for any corporation and for the American business system is not—and never has been—an economic measure. It is a political judgment about which economic rules and structures make sense.

The Long-Standing Question of Social Legitimacy

As one traces back the ideological foundations of American society, the impressive thing is not that there has been such great concern about corporate governance, but that in a sense there has been so little. Business has evolved by initiative and experiment. It never had an overwhelmingly clear endorsement as a social institution. The idea of allowing individuals to joust with one another in pursuit of personal profit was an exciting and romantic one when it was first proposed as a way of correcting other problems in society; but over time, its ugly side and potential for abuse became apparent. The zest for competition carried with it temptations to subvert its discipline or exploit its limits. Single-minded, short-term pressure for financial results did not encourage business or its neighbors to think through longer-range consequences of decisions (any more than frequent elections encourage such thinking in government). The "invisible hand" that governed market transactions had more appeal to customers whose needs it served than to employees whose job security was threatened by marketplace rejections.

THE TENSION BETWEEN ENTREPRENEURIAL FREEDOM AND PERSONAL RESPONSIBILITY

Adam Smith was concerned enough to discuss the issues in a second book. While *The Wealth of Nations* argued strongly for the advantages of letting a businessman concentrate on his own self-interest, *The Theory of Moral Sentiments* argued equally fervently that given the choice between private gain and public service, there are times when the responsible businessman must choose the second, not the first. As the abuses and imbalances became more evident, criticism of the capitalist model became more frequent. Even before the Civil War, George Fitzhugh, a Southerner eloquent in his defense of slavery, wrote that "the virtues" of competitive Northern capitalism had "lost all their loveliness." In much sharper tones, European writers like Karl Marx were not only criticizing the system but were suggesting a night-and-day alternative. They argued for replacement of capitalism by a system which built on the good side— the selfless, communal, generous side—of man's nature and maximized social welfare by reinforcing those qualities rather than aggressiveness and greed. They viewed the ideology and the early progress of European capitalism as a path toward permanent exploitation and subjugation of the working classes.

Competitive capitalism assumes a model of man that is a permanent—and to many, an increasing—irritant in sustaining public tolerance and support for business. It is not only a stimulus to attacks on the corporation in university lecture halls and church pulpits, but it is a, damper on the confidence of business executives to explain and defend the system. A system which encourages and rewards selfishness, whatever good results it generally produces for society, is bound to suffer embarrassing excesses. It is often hard to explain that risk without seeming to endorse the abuses. It is difficult to defend the trade-offs that a paper or chemical company must weigh between profits and pollution control without seeming to support a firm that refused to take even basic measures for environmental protection, or to herald the accomplishments of some firms in product quality without also acknowledging that the market also supports manufacturers of shoddy products.

One reason for low confidence in business is distrust of what executives say. Sometimes, by a tradition which restrains criticism of peers or by advice of counsel, executives appear in public to condone actions which they clearly view privately as unacceptable in ethics or in result. Other times, they advertise standards which, it turns out, their organizations are not meeting. The public found it implausible that top electrical company executives were unaware of price-fixing actions some years ago, and finds it implausible now that executives have not known more than many have admitted about bribes and sales commissions paid to government officials overseas. Few executives have defended questionable payments aggressively in public, even though privately many still view them as absolutely necessary in many markets.

The public wants credible explanations as well as ethical behavior. Candid rogues are sometimes more respected than silent cowards or pious hypocrites.

THE ARTIFICIALITY OF ECONOMIC GROUND RULES

The other two major strains in capitalist ideology come from the idea that only economic return to shareholders counts in judging corporate performance and that, to avoid "pie-in-the-sky" evaluations, measures of return should stress short-term results. Adam Smith argued this as cleanly in his day as Friedrich Hayek and Milton Friedman have in ours. As rules of the game, these are precise; and we know from experience they are beneficial rules in services provided for society. If we dilute these by allowing social as well as economic objectives or by making vague rather than hardheaded allowances for long-range contingencies, we are in the position of trying to decide who has won a game of chess after rules on how the pieces should move have been abolished.

Classical capitalist economic doctrine is not oblivious to other goals that society wants to achieve, but it assumes—and assumes emphatically—that society will be better off if the businessman keeps his eye on profit and if social questions are resolved outside the corporation by the processes of government. If society wants limits on profit-seeking to ensure clean air or job security, let voters get legislators to act. Then have legislators impose whatever constraints are necessary, hopefully using some imagination to create incentives and penalties for compliance that will take advantage of, rather than frustrate or ignore the corporation's drive for financial return. Within the constraints, though, keep that drive focused and uncomplicated by other goals.

Some people—far more in Europe than in the United States—oppose this idea because they fundamentally disagree with the capitalistic approach. Their ideal for improved governance is not minor tinkering, but in the Marxian tradition, wholesale shifts of enterprises from decentralized private to state ownership and from focus on profits to focus on achievement of governmentally determined economic and social plans.

Most of those, however, who are urging corporations to mix social and economic objectives believe they are friends of private enterprise. They would still keep economic objectives uppermost, but they believe that corporations (and all institutions in society) share with government the difficult problem of defining and achieving social objectives, too. Some see this as a necessary condition for sustaining social legitimacy for the corporation; and others, who appear to be critics, are really flatterers. They want greater corporate involvement in curbing pollution, training minorities, or improving the quality of urban life because they trust businessmen to do the job better than government.

Many with these views, to the chagrin of some of their tutors in conservative economics departments, work within the executive suites of major companies. Directors and managers do not all sit comfortably with the discovery that a new chemical process, which offers product or cost advantages, has created a long-term health hazard for workers, or that clear new drives for job opportunities by minorities and women are blocked by supervisory attitudes and seniority rules within the firm. They may, to some critics, still overemphasize the profit dimension; but many think about how to mix economic and social objectives in order to be at peace with themselves, with their families, and with their associates and friends.

The advantages of specializing organizations and individuals to perform economic tasks in society are intellectually clear, but the desires to make individuals and organizations rounded microcosms of society's concerns have a compelling human dimension. The chief pressures do come from outside the firm, but some of the urge toward social responsibility comes from within.

THE CORPORATION AS AN UNANTICIPATED RESULT
OF COMPETITIVE CAPITALISM

Another issue of legitimacy is the question of whether today's corporation and marketplace look enough like the original free enterprise model to be recognizable under that label. At first glance, the evidence is not encouraging. All authorities, before 1840, on rights and privileges for corporations are suspect because they had no inkling of what a modern corporation would be like. Until then, most firms were small—single unit, single location, a few products, local markets. The owner was also likely to be the day-by-day manager, with at most one level of supervision between himself and the workers. As much as the owner in such a setting pursued a goal of profit maximization, he was also directly and personally subject to other, subtler social controls because of close links with suppliers, customers, workers, and the community surrounding the firm.

Not until after 1840 was there significant growth in multiunit organizations for which owners began to build layers of middle-level, salaried managers to run the business. By 1900, after national rail and telegraph networks had developed, there was a new spurt of growth: by vertical integration to control supplies of raw materials and to assume direct responsibility for developing markets which a firm's expanded production capacity enabled it to serve and, less successfully, by horizontal merger across product and geographic lines. Both moves required new levels of discipline and skill in the arts of management.

Corporations as we know them today really did not begin to take their present form until after World War I. Then, professional managers like Alfred P. Sloan, Jr. at General Motors showed a knack for making very large production and marketing systems work. The biggest firms spanned several combinations of products and markets. We began to see not only new applications of technology, new tables of organization, and new techniques for decision and control; but also a vision of the enterprise as a strategic unit, setting goals analytically and moving systematically to achieve them in a changing competitive environment. Behind the concept of strategy was an aggressive commitment to growth and a presumption, by adroit shifting of products and markets, of corporate immortality.

By the 1930s big companies were known more by the managers who led them than by the owners for whom the profits were supposedly being pursued. As A.A. Berle and Gardner Means documented, ownership became more widely dispersed and shareholders far removed from active participation in management. Large corporate organizations, led by professional specialists and managers, lived partly by the laws of economics and partly by the dictates of bureaucracy.

Corporations developed still further after World War II. With relative political stability on the international scene, further advances in transportation and communication services, continued innovation in the arts of management, and a zest for growth and permanence, companies expanded in the United States and established large operations overseas. Old companies blossomed, as RCA did with the introduction of television; IBM, with the advent of computers; and the automobile companies, with affluent consumers at home and new markets abroad. Entirely new companies like Litton Industries and Control Data emerged and flourished. Huge multiproduct, multimarket conglomerates appeared, and although many failed, some like ITT and Textron have had great success.

The biggest firms have great political as well as economic leverage. With planning and investment horizons that extend many years ahead, decisions today often carry important and irreversible long-run consequences. The concentration of market share within industries and the cost for entry of new players are a far cry from the kind of open competitive system which Smith and other contemporary political economists had tried to prescribe.

Economists like George Stigler and Milton Friedman, staunch advocates of the private enterprise system, join Galbraith and other less sure defenders in questioning the degree to which large corporations have found ways to shelter themselves from market forces.

In most major industries, even though there may not be grounds for antitrust action, there is enough concentration of market share and enough question of whether increased size and scope of operations have brought efficiency and benefits for consumers that periodic antitrust review is warranted. Economic studies have not supported many big company claims of economies of scale in research and innovation, in minimization of costs, in efficient distribution of goods and services, or in responsiveness to changing environmental challenges.

It was, after all, a Republican president, Dwight Eisenhower, and not an unfriendly radical who warned about the dangers of overly cozy business-government relationships through a "military-industrial" complex. The leading opponents of deregulation for many industries turn out to be executives of the companies and leaders of the unions who would be affected. Firms in serious trouble like Penn Central and Lockheed have had no embarrassment about seeking federal insulation from defeats in the marketplace.

The old ideology simply does not allow the blanket endorsement which many corporate leaders would like to have from society for their current operations. In size, in ownership, in scope and impact of operations, in market structures, and in present relationships to government, today's corporation is vastly different from anything that writers had in mind 200 years ago. Present grants of social legitimacy for the corporation must come from present performance and from appropriately revised descriptions and assurances about how the system is supposed to work for society's benefit.

MARKET VERSUS POLITICAL FREEDOM

The final persistent challenge to legitimacy comes from a long-standing, unresolved confusion about the American commitment to rights of property versus rights of man. In the early enthusiasm for capitalism and democracy, the two seemed to go together, especially when the first practical interpretations of democracy gave the vote only to white male property-holders. But feelings of divergence grew as industrial expansion carried with it casualness about damage to the environment and about exploitation of immigrant labor. As management hierarchies developed, they were more authoritarian for the sake of unity and efficiency than they were democratic.

The model of man reflected in Frederick Taylor's specifications of movements for the "pig iron handler" or parodied by Charlie Chaplin in *Modern Times* had little to do with "life, liberty, and the pursuit of happiness." However, by providing jobs at all and by making needed goods and services widely and inexpensively available, industry created, even for many of the people it seemed to exploit, a feeling of life, liberty, and happiness off the job. Despite the signs of conflict, democracy and business expansion still seemed basically in harmony.

But now expectations are higher, and evidence of major structural problems is more clear. Business itself has encouraged the idea of shareholder democracy, of consumer sovereignty, and of employee rights to "participate" in management. Both the desire and the capability of such groups to assert influence have been improved by advances in educational opportunities and the opportunity, with security about food and shelter, to spend life trying to satisfy higher level aspirations. For both the educational opportunity and the shift in aspirations, the past contributions of business to developing the economy deserve great credit. Business has promised to be more open and has helped create a public which is articulate about making new demands.

Thus, having spent decades trumpeting (and proving) prowess in design and technology, automobile companies should not be surprised to find the public expecting miracles in improving the safety or energy efficiency of new cars. Companies which advertised the importance of quality when American products were better than sleazily-made imports cannot expect consumer sympathy when others beat us at the quality game. Shareholders encouraged to vote on management proposals can easily come to believe that democracy includes proxy initiatives about investment in South Africa or representation of women and minorities on boards of directors. Employees encouraged to make suggestions of a relatively minor sort to improve their motivation and productivity naturally find ways to use the same channels to raise more basic questions about working conditions and job security.

Corporations have been democratic to the extent of offering to let the market and the society judge them by results, but they have jealously guarded management's right to set direction, to plan, and to decide on major courses of action without a great deal of external participation or feedback. Such freedom of initiative represents both the essence of property rights and the essence of the flexibility and the capacity for coordinated action that has made American businesses very efficient producers of goods and services. With such discretion, though, goes tremendous power, not only to achieve important and useful results, but along the way to create destructive side consequences and even to persuade the government away from giving proper attention to public welfare.

The pressures are on for more democracy in planning what a corporation will undertake, and observers from many points on the political spectrum are raising anew the question of whether economic freedom for the large corporation and political and personal freedom for the individual citizen can fit together. On one hand, some corporate executives talk wistfully about how much easier it is to do business in a friendly dictatorship such as Brazil or Iran than it is to handle continuing challenges to their autonomy and judgment in the United States. In a recent essay, two economists, Michael Jensen and William Meckling, have weighed the importance of preserving property rights versus unrestricted freedoms of speech and the press and come down solidly on the side of the former. Although they do not propose specific alternatives, they believe that our present form of representative government will lead inevitably to the death of the private corporation and to the curtailment of economic freedoms for the individual.

Somewhere in the middle, in a thoughtful book called *Politics and Markets,* Charles Lindblom worries:

> Enormously large, rich in resources, the big corporations . . . command more resources than do most government units. They can also, over a broad range, insist that government meet their demands, even if these demands run counter to those of citizens. . . . Moreover, they do not disqualify themselves from playing the partisan role of a citizen . . . and they exercise unusual veto powers. . . . The large private corporation fits oddly into democratic theory and vision. Indeed, it does not fit.

Writers like Karl Hess in *Dear America* and E. F. Schumacher in *Small is Beautiful* argue strongly that dismemberment of large organizations into smaller units is our only hope for preserving freedom and preventing a slide toward a fascistic society.

It is fair to argue, as many businessmen do, that democracy does not exist except in societies which have decentralized, market-oriented structures for their economies. Unfortunately, it does not therefore follow that where a market system of private enterprise exists, democracy will survive. Economic freedom may have been necessary for political freedoms to flower, but evidence from around the world suggests that economic freedoms do not always work to keep political freedom in force.

Thus, there is conflict in our heritage which clouds and confuses the place of the large corporation in society. Whatever roots the corporation can claim in the great debates about social organization which took place in the eighteenth century, those roots lie chiefly in discussions of how best to organize economic activity. The other discussions, which put a Bill of Rights into our Constitution and which created legal protections for individual citizens against oppressive power from any source, did a great deal to insure evolution of public challenges to the corporation. General Motors and stock options are no more inherently American than Ralph Nader or the class action suit. Both business and opposition to business are as American as apple pie.

Disappointments in Corporate Performance

As questions of legitimacy and governance have evolved, today's debate centers around three factors: corporate *performance*, corporate *power*, and new aspirations for *professionalism* in management. Performance has four dimensions. How well does an enterprise do in achieving the basic things that it sets out to do and that it advertises as its primary contributions to the public weal? How good are its results along the economic dimensions of profits, return on investment, and payout to shareholders by which it has primarily asked to be judged? Do the actions of an enterprise add to or detract from the general public regard for business as a social institution? Do they contribute to some of the broader social goals that elements of society are asking that businesses pursue along with economic objectives?

Note that only two of these questions have primarily a social as opposed to an economic focus or assume that the corporation needs do anything but try to maximize profits. Corporate governance is an issue today because business has disappointed in its primary role as well as in some of the new and controversial roles that society is pressing on it.

BASIC FAILURES OF SERVICE

To steal a line from *The New Yorker* after the great Northeast power failure of 1965: ". . . we were learning that we really didn't have to believe—as we would have thought we did—that someone, somewhere, knows what is going on." With society's blessing, business has created an economy of almost inconceivable complexity in its requirements for smoothly functioning technology and human organization. Corporations have not been bashful about advertising their accomplishments. When everything works well, we stand in awe; but when the system breaks down, business takes the blame.

Politicians find it attractive to suggest publicly-owned alternatives to Consolidated Edison, for example, but not because it is demonstrably inefficient or socially irresponsible. Still, having been at the center of two major regional power failures and having not yet fully mastered the organizational and technological details of handling inquiries and complaints from their millions of customers on a timely, individualized basis, they have left an impression of ineptness in management. The same was true for New York Telephone when they underestimated the demands for growth in service during the late 1960s, but they were able to improve their image dramatically by the way they recovered from a disastrous fire and interruption of service a few years later.

Just as public schools which cannot teach children to read become public jokes, companies which build high expectations for products and services are judged harshly when performance falls short. When an automobile company admits that competitive pressures have led someone in middle management to fake environmental test results, or when journalists can diagnose the series of missteps which led to a tragic design flaw in a new aircraft as unfortunate failures of organizational control rather than as callousness or stupidity, outside intervention or supervision of management may seem the obvious remedy for internal management failings.

More because the public would like to believe what managers say about their capabilities rather than because they instinctively mistrust them, the public has assumed that pharmaceutical companies with sophisticated research laboratories could avoid putting dangerous drugs on the market, that chemical companies would not be surprised as often as they seem to be by harmful pollution or hygienic effects of their operations, and that food companies would not be subject to basic challenges on the nutritional values of their products. The public holds accountants in higher esteem than they do lawyers and doctors but have what many CPAs believe are unreasonable expectations about the abilities of an audit team to detect and expose corporate fraud.

It is convenient to blame antibusiness feelings among affluent college students on the radicalism of their professors, but in my observations, more of such feelings arise from personal frustrations as young consumers, "gut" reactions to early experience as employees, resentment at disruptions in family life that their fathers' corporate careers have caused, and absorption of bitter comments they have heard their elders make about the pressures and ethics of organizational life. They are at a stage in life when idealistic ideologies appeal, but their attitudes often have greater anchoring in experience.

What does all this have to do with governance? Before wrestling with nuances of economic or social performance, the key issue for any organization that wants to avoid intrusions on how it manages its affairs is whether it can and does deliver the basic things it is in business to provide and that, by general expectation and its own advertising, it has promised to provide. Where, for technological or organizational reasons, the reach of private enterprise exceeds its grasp, it may be less vulnerable to adverse public reactions if it shares—in advance—perspective on what the limits are.

ECONOMIC DIMENSIONS OF PERFORMANCE

Some of the most persistent pressures for changes in governance and many of the major legislated changes, from antitrust to abolition of fixed commissions in the securities industry, have had as their primary objective improved performance of businesses as economic institutions. Long before dissidents began appearing at shareholders' meetings to protest employment policies or investments overseas, others had been making the rounds to press on issues like cumulative voting for directors, dividend rates, and limits on executive stock options. Their goal was to redress shareholders' rights against self-assumed prerogatives of management and to increase management's drive to show good profits.

Many proposals for reform have primarily an economic motivation. Most of the current pressures for clarification of accounting standards, for some form of inflation accounting, and for disclosure of earnings forecasts are designed to make it easier for investors to evaluate the true economic condition and potential of firms in different industries. Proposals to make it easier for shareholders to engage in proxy battles with management and to give them a fighting chance to outvote management have arisen because companies have missed economic as much as social opportunities. In 1978 the Securities and Exchange Commission investigated the rights of management to "go private" by buying back stock or to refuse to let shareholders vote on takeover bids because in certain instances such actions seem a perversion of management's primary economic obligation to shareholders.

Even many of the proposed reforms for boards of directors—more outsiders, clearer separation of board and management roles, possibilities of independent staff for directors—make as much sense as devices to increase corporate profits as they do for drawing attention toward other kinds of goals. One sees this perhaps most clearly in changes that have already taken place in rules for directors of mutual funds. All these changes force the director toward a much more aggressive role in holding down the costs of fund management and in making sure that investment decisions are made strictly with a view of maximizing achievement of the fund's investment objectives.

Some forms of government regulation have been undertaken to make markets more competitive than private business interests now want. For airlines, for trucking, and for the securities industry, the talk is of "deregulation" or "reregulation." The hope is that by giving individual enterprises greater discretion about the mix of services and prices they offer and by allowing freer play of market forces, efficiencies will be achieved and some pockets of monopoly profits will be eliminated. It has been an instructive exercise to see government encourage more open price and service competition and vigorous advocates of "free enterprise" resist the changes, but these examples suggest that not all the ferment in corporate governance is leading toward a stronger governmental role.

Economic performance is likely to remain a significant element in discussion of governance reform. As much as management believes it is dedicated only to the pursuit of profits, studies of decision making and performance in large corporate bureaucracies suggest that—absent pressure from directors and shareholders—many factors blunt and divert that drive, especially with managements that do not have significant ownership stakes or that do not face tough competitive conditions. The realization that a large percentage of leading companies, despite glowing reports in some cases to shareholders, have not been earning enough after allowance for inflation to replenish capital has to become a major societal issue. Economic performance is corporate management's primary job, and if management slips, it is society's challenge to find ways to get them back on the track.

THE CREDIBILITY OF BUSINESS AS AN INSTITUTION

The one area of governance reform for which most of the pressure may be coming from within business itself relates to steps that will protect the overall image and credibility of large corporations as social institutions. Certain kinds of performance mean little to the individual firm, but do influence greatly how society views the wisdom and legitimacy of all private corporate enterprise.

An early example of this is the effort to restrain deceptive advertising and marketing practices. Corporations gave support to private regulatory efforts like the Better Business Bureaus and the National Advertising Review Board because abuses by some firms were reducing trust in business generally. Whatever their public stance, many responsible advertisers welcomed at least the advent of the Federal Trade Commission and of local consumer protection agencies because these promised oversight and control of the most brazen offenders beyond what any private group, without legal sanctions, could accomplish.

Groups setting standards for precision and quality in manufacturing have had similar origins. While some standards may have been established as an indirect way to control and limit competition, there is no question that much of the effort was sincerely motivated to give consumers assurances about products that individual companies, in the absence of such standards, would be tempted to undermine. Again, while much standard setting is done in the private sector, business has acquiesced in government intervention where greater degrees of discipline were required.

Similar debate has developed around "questionable payments," both the problems which have arisen from illegal political contributions and those which have arisen from bribes and exorbitant sales commissions to public officials in pursuit of government contracts. Despite the traumatic turnover in management that has been forced at companies like Lockheed and Gulf Oil, revelation of the payments has not seemed to have major effects on public willingness to buy or use their products. Nevertheless, despite conflicting evidence, revelation of the payments may have had a marked negative impact on public trust of business in general.

Business as well as the public, therefore, is concerned about how to find rules not only to discipline management behavior better but also to limit future exposure to damaging public reaction. One avenue of response has been formulation or reformulation of codes of conduct for the individual enterprise. Another has been discussion across firm and industry lines by groups such as the Conference Board and the Business Roundtable about general improvements which should be made to codes of conduct or to private supervising authorities, such as boards of directors. A third has been examination within such groups as the American Bar Association and the American Institute of Certified Public Accountants of the responsibilities that legal counsel and auditors must assume. While the current disposition of business is to try to prevent future Lockheed or Gulf Oil scandals as much as possible by private rather than governmental initiatives, executives may help shape public action to control abuses that private regulation does not reach.

When general public confidence is at stake, whatever the cause, corporate managers have strong incentives to collaborate on private remedies or to acquiesce in public control measures.

DEMANDS FOR SOCIAL AS WELL AS ECONOMIC PERFORMANCE

Beyond pressures for economic performance and for behavior—including ethical behavior—that will reinforce social legitimacy for the corporation, there are significant expectations for social performance by corporations. These demands suggest many ideas for change in corporate governance.

Such social pressures, as the opening quotations from J. M. Clark showed, are not a new phenomenon. Companies have seen—and survived—the abolition of child labor, governmental endorsement of labor's right to organize, pure food and drug legislation, a minimum wage act, and many other moves that seemed at the time to threaten their continued existence as independent economic entities.

Yet not until recently has it become fashionable to talk in depth about the social responsibilities of business; to equate consumers, environmentalists, and new claimants for employment opportunities with shareholders as "stakeholders" in the enterprise; or to suggest among mathematical economists that equation systems for maximizing profits might have to be rewritten to satisfy some "multicriterion objective function."

Until a few years ago, models for corporate strategic planning clearly gave primary emphasis to profit and return-on-investment objectives. All other considerations were simply regarded as "planning constraints." Now, conversations with planners in both American and European companies indicate that, more and more, noneconomic considerations are at least beginning to be considered as objectives. At an extreme, the planner for a major German company made it plain that for his organization, the primary objective now was to provide near-term job security. Only secondarily did they seek to make enough money to assure the firm's long-term survival. Economic objectives still dominate social objectives for most firms, but from a combination of external pressure and internal preference, they no longer provide a rationale for comfortably setting social issues aside.

Some social questions—pollution control, product reliability, health and safety in the workplace, employment effects of multinational operations—have come to the fore because as social problems they are largely the direct by-product of business pursuit of economic goals. The fouling of rivers may have been endorsed by customers seeking cheap steel or cheap paper or by communities eager to attract industry and keep jobs. But once those customers and communities say—or let others say—that the river needs to be cleaned up, they put the burden back on business to decide how the trade-offs will be made and the job will be done.

Pursuit of immediate profits has trapped business into many decisions with side consequences that are viewed negatively by groups outside, sometimes immediately and sometimes years later. Often, as in the case of many environmental or industrial health situations, outside groups are no more aware than corporate management is at the time of decision what those negative eventualities may be. However, the eventual costs are heavy enough that society is demanding corporations run themselves—or be regulated—to reduce these future risks.

We currently do not know which approaches make most sense. Many demands still are for proscriptive regulation, which tends to respond to yesterday's mistakes and to limit capability to pursue either economic or social objectives flexibly in the future. Other demands are for public planning or technology assessment, with the hope that somehow these will prove more farsighted and socially responsible than private efforts. Some seek changes in the outlook and decision premises of company directors and of both top and middle management as the only way to achieve a better balance between short-term economic gains and long-term social costs, and some have imaginative proposals for using the legal system (class action suits, prison terms for irresponsible management decisions, etc.) or the market system (tax incentives, subsidies, etc.) to get results.

A second category of social issues does not arise as a side consequence of business actions, but because business has to be involved in helping to realize the new goals. Examples would include the drive to open job opportunities for minorities and women, some aspects of environmental improvement (such as litter reduction) which go beyond problems that business alone has created, many elements of urban renewal, and the move toward national independence and higher standards of living in the developing countries.

Here the pressures on business to adopt new goals may be most intense; yet the conservatism of managers about responding to pressures at the expense of economic performance may be most valid. Society, not business, has responsibility for deciding whether Rhodesia should be recognized and how cities should be preserved. Corporate managements which try to lead the way risk being slapped down for acting in presumptive fashion and risk losing the support of both employees and customers in the process. Yet by the time society has given a clear signal for new patterns of behavior, the corporation risks looking like a laggard and may have to be forced into conformity by legislation, as in the case of equal employment opportunity laws.

Because neither business nor society can easily predict the side consequences of business actions which are likely to call for socially-oriented response and because the flow of social aspirations requiring business participation for realization is ever-changing, the important issues of corporate governance are general, not specific. Society worries too much about designing and implementing speci-

fic controls on corporate behavior and too little, with acknowledge-
ment that corporations will be judged in both economic and social
terms, about looking for general ways to redirect the attentions of
directors and managers. Solutions must be flexible to meet tomor-
row's needs as well as today's.

Questions of Power over Resources and People

If performance questions have provided one stream of pressures on corporate governance, a second stream of pressures derives
from the continuing argument over powers that large corporations
have accumulated. In available capital and human talent, as we have
mentioned, a company like Exxon or IBM dwarfs all but the very
largest of national government organizations. In political clout,
more than many people would like, major companies have been
able to decide important legislation—even sometimes the fate of national governments. Although businessmen like to bemoan the
power of unions (and remind us that they also speak for the interests
of their employees), many reasonably neutral analysts have rated
management's influence in American politics as substantially greater
than labor's.

Size, wealth, and political influence—as much as Americans endorse the struggle to win them—are suspect once they have been
attained. Big business is under attack to a large extent simply because it *is* big and because our entire social and political tradition
warns us to beware concentrations of power. Big business, as many
corporate executives realize, is not always even popular with small
business, and small businessmen have been behind some restrictive
kinds of corporate legislation. Public tolerance of labor unions and
of a huge governmental apparatus is not generally based on a
greater liking for these institutions, but on conviction that countervailing centers of power are needed to hold corporations in line.

Bigness faces increased hostility because of the new surge of emphasis in society on individual rights and freedoms. Even among
critics of the corporation a generation ago there would not have
been as much tolerance as there is now for individual challenges to
the way in which corporations work: for workers who flagrantly disregard work schedules and work discipline, for "whistle-blowers"
who make public corporate problems and errors, for organizers of
demonstrations or class action suits, for people—like clever computer

embezzlers—who outfox the company, and even, unfortunately, for the terrorists who have made their mark by kidnapping executives in Western Europe and Latin America.

Power is an issue to the individual because it is not always available, to the degree promised, in the marketplace or the voting booth. Customers have a choice to buy or not to buy, but the menu of product options often depends more on what companies want to offer than on what customers would like to have. Business cherishes a right to create as well as to find and satisfy demand. It is ironic—and alarming—that in a society where consumer preferences are studied and served to a degree not seen in most other countries of the world, a customers' movement to protest serious corporate and governmental disregard of their wants has become a powerful social and political force. Companies and legislators who find themselves surprised by this development need to go back to basics of what they intend by customer and voter service.

Power, to some degree, is an ideological matter, much more so in Western Europe than in the United States. The place of the corporation here is still basically supported by a belief in private property and by a suspicion of central government which outweighs most fears about business. American unions use their power in Congress to improve their position at the bargaining table, not to achieve a share of owning or running companies.

However, in Western Europe a quite different situation prevails. There the debate between private and public ownership is intense and long-standing. To many Europeans, giving government more power in order to take over and manage major companies seems worth the risk. Within both public and private companies in Europe, the most aggressive new claimant for influence over managerial planning and decision-making is not the consumer. It is the employee. Some combination of union and direct employee representation on boards of directors is now well established in Germany, Sweden, the Netherlands, and Ireland. It seems only a matter of time until it becomes a reality in Great Britain, and it is under active consideration in France and Italy as well.

Some of the pressures for change involve, rather than controversy over distribution of power, concern about parallelism in how it is exercised. As government sets up regulatory structures to deal with business, the corporation must reflect these in its own structures and procedures. As corporations have grown in size and in claims to permanence, and as they and society have focused more on the lives of individuals within, there is more talk about "constitutions" for the corporation and about "due process" for its employees. These are meant to resemble what exist for society as a whole. Legal and political considerations are likely to compete with hierarchical assumptions in future decisions about organizational design.

Finally, in one sense, there are some pressures to give corporations more power than they now have—and more than many would like to have. We have discussed the degree to which society has looked to corporations to help achieve social goals, such as employment opportunities for blacks and women, which cannot be achieved without business help. In such situations, advocates of social change look at corporations not only for what they can do within their own boundaries, but for what they can do by using influence or diverting resources to get cooperation from other companies or from other kinds of institutions in society. Individuals and groups with many "causes" have sought to exercise the proxy process (to pass resolutions or place representatives on a board) and to solicit contributions of money and manpower so that the corporation's affiliation would magnify what they could accomplish alone. One of the most bothersome issues about increasing "shareholder democracy" is how to keep resulting initiatives focused on things a corporation really ought to do and away from things where it would simply—and inappropriately—be magnifying a dissident voice in place of support that voters or legislators will not give.

Professionalism as a Stimulus to Governance Reform

It is perhaps only a minor factor, but it seems worth speculating a little on the degree to which the current interest in reform of corporate governance stems from an "itch" by highly-trained people in business, government, the media, and the universities to tinker with more complex concepts of organizational design. There is no question that many individuals who care about the future of corporations would be happier if they were less restricted to a narrow economic rationale for their existence and less hamstrung by legalistic regulations that did not square with the dynamics—economic, organizational, and technological—of making a complex organization work. Executives would like to be known for better-rounded performance. Government lawyers would like to be known for more constructive approaches to social control. Business school professors would like to stop trying to justify purely economic rationales for corporate existence to their colleagues in other disciplines.

All three recognize that, even without the extreme deference to employees shown in Western Europe, corporations which perform badly are less likely to disappear than in years past. If pressures from both customers and employees limit the market's ability to do away with weaker companies, management and government have an ever larger responsibility to reform and rebuild them. To a greater extent than businessmen have acknowledged so far, the burden of reform is one that they have conceived and assumed for themselves out of a belief that they ought to try and out of a confidence that new and higher levels of organization for business and society can be achieved.

The Heart of the Governance Debate

Changing what a corporation attempts presumes some agreement about what the directions of change need to be or, failing that, some agreement about who besides management should represent society in the search. Changing what a company achieves requires more than exhortations. It requires a combination of plans and actions that will move a multimillion or multibillion dollar complex of people and machines to work together in different ways. No simple instruction will be heeded if the air is full of competing suggestions and demands, and no simple instruction without development and follow-through to make it work can assure a desired shift in outcomes. The debate on governance involves both questions of direction and of means for accomplishing results.

QUESTIONS OF DIRECTION

There are two major barriers to deciding what we want to try to achieve. Performance goals are hard to specify and to relate, one to another; and concepts of power and rights are enough confused within society that it is hard to resolve which goals should have priority.

We have had a great deal of practice in learning to specify and measure economic performance, but even into this area of relatively sure measurement, important new concepts have been introduced in recent years. Simple notions of break-even points and pay-back period have given way to analysis of discounted cash flows and sophisticated concepts of return on investment. We know more about how to handle costs of capital and probabilistic allowances for risk and uncertainty, and we are searching for better ways to reconcile accounting measures and economic concepts of profit in an age of continuing inflation. Since long-range profitability calls for different decisions sometimes than short-term profit maximization would, we would like ways to make long-term measures more meaningful as guides to planning and action. There are still analytic uncertainties about where to head even if management and society only had interest in economic accomplishments for the corporation.

With measures of social performance, the analytic problem is many times worse. Suppose we agree that it is a good thing, in general, to curb pollution or to reorganize routine factory and office operations so that employees get more satisfaction from their work. How do we list and eventually quantify costs and benefits of possible actions so that we can make intelligent choices and exercise sensible control over use of scarce human and material resources? If we expect management to balance and integrate economic and social performance objectives, they must eventually be able to specify them in comparable terms.

In a world where "zero defect" conditions are either literally impossible or prohibitively expensive to achieve, how can we determine analytically when accomplishments that are clearly less than ideal are, nonetheless, sufficient. The idea of maximizing profits—even if that is what companies try to do—has never been an absolute. Maximization has always meant achievement within limits of available resources and wisdom and within the formal and informal constraints that society has placed on corporate operations. Efforts to maximize any kind of social performance are subject to the same limits on resources, wisdom, and societal tolerance. Further, any proposal that corporations should maximize combined performance on a mix of economic and social goals does not mean that each will be achieved at highest levels. It means the reverse: that because of interest in a balanced menu of results, something will have to be sacrificed along each individual dimension of performance. Balance means trade-offs, and it greatly complicates the analytic challenge both to corporations and to those who try to evaluate them from outside.

Analytic problems can be solved, at least in part. As demand for progress increases, we will get better measures and models for planning and auditing social performance. But to focus on the need for better measures obscures the larger problem. Society has not yet sorted out what improvements in social performance it expects. There are, as the following chapter describes, wide disagreements about priorities among different constituents or "stakeholders" of the corporation: investors, customers, workers, the professional managers who lead them, victims of side-effects of corporate economic decisions (neighbors harmed by pollution, small businesses doomed by a plant closing, etc.), agencies of government or private social action groups who want corporate help in achieving their goals, and all of these replicated across national and cultural boundaries for the multinational firm and across future generations if one thinks about long-range and perhaps irreversible consequences of some corporate decisions. Because the current atmosphere encourages all such groups to approach the corporation as advocates rather than as balancers, accurate assessment of what they want is even more difficult.

Individual citizens themselves in our complex society are walking contradictions in their thoughts and actions toward corporate goals. John Doe, steelworker, will curse management for working conditions and for not approaching government sooner about protection against imports. Yet he will also protest higher prices for food if migrant farm workers were to be brought anywhere near his level of earnings and higher prices for clothing if textile import barriers were imposed. Sally Smith, activist, grumbles about the failure of local banks to make more loans in slum areas, but moves her savings account around regularly from bank to bank to take advantage of premium offers and small differences in interest rates. All the people across the country who want more social responsibility gave very poor response to the idea of mutual funds that would limit investments to highly ethical, socially responsible companies. Corporations have difficulty making balanced choices that individuals trying to assert influence will not make for themselves.

Even if groups and individuals knew what mix they wanted, there are important questions about how to let them vote. Our society opens several avenues for influence, none of which was specifically designed to facilitate governance of corporate performance on social issues. The market as voting place was intended not as a structure for influencing social performance, but as a way of expressing reactions to particular offerings of goods, services, or contractual relationships. An automobile company cannot reliably decide, as Ford Motor once did, that customers who refuse to pay extra for a safety package are thus not interested in improved safety in the cars they buy. The proxy process for shareholders was not designed as an effective channel for measuring how even shareholders feel about pollution abatement or trade with dictatorships overseas. It certainly was not meant to let activists buy in by small shareholdings to obtain a forum for social dissent. Unions have evolved as powerful forces for negotiations of wages and working conditions, but not as effectively democratic structures for representing employee interests in the management of individual firms.

The press and television have become more aggressive in analysis and advocacy on corporate behavior, but business can properly raise questions about whether the media as profit-seeking organizations themselves have not limited what they report and how they report in ways which make them distorting and divisive influences in society's effort to resolve complex issues. The same can be said for the role which society allows to lawyers and entrepreneurial social action groups. Dealing with business, they are often far better at lying down across the tracks than in suggesting better ways to drive the train.

Actions by government, reflecting different assessments by legislators and administrators of what the voting citizenry wants, also have been characterized by fragmentation and confusion. Differences in how states charter or tax corporations or how they legislate against roadside litter give very different signals about what different parts of the country want companies to do. One of the informal duties assumed by the New York regional head of the Federal Trade Commission has been to help decide which of various questions and complaints about business should be routed to each of the seventeen different but overlapping federal, state, and local consumer protection agencies in the metropolitan area. Even within the federal government, the Departments of State and Defense, the Internal Revenue Service, the Securities and Exchange Commission, and Congress have pushed large multinational corporations in conflicting directions, as they sort out what should be done about bribes and political payments overseas.

Businessmen know that the game they play requires strong officiating. But on a gridiron with a thousand referees, no one can be sure if—or where—to throw the ball.

QUESTIONS OF REMEDIES

With uncertainties about goals and power relationships, reform of corporate governance involves more than direction and controls for business. The first focus for reform, in fact, is essentially *educational*: to assure a flow of information from corporations—directly and through groups like analysts, advocacy groups, and the press who can add useful commentary—to help the public at large decide what new goals business should follow. As a better educated and more concerned public has sought more information about corporate aspirations and performance, disclosure requirements have been expanded; and still new kinds of openness may be beneficial.

There is a need for improvements in explanation and interpretation both by the groups who want to make major shifts in how corporations behave and by those who would prefer, at most, refinements and enhancements to traditional roles. The desired outcome for society is a world in which individual citizens and advocacy groups are at least considering the same range of factors and alternatives that a responsible executive must review, even though their values and thought processes lead them to different conclusions.

The educational process must run in the other direction, too. Information about society's values, perceptions, and attitudes must flow better than it often does to directors, executives, and even to others much lower in the corporate hierarchy. Executives who had explored the range of possible public reactions to disclosure of bribes or illegal political contributions would have been, at the least, less likely to go ahead with them. As only a handful of companies now do in systematic ways, business needs to begin asking society how they will respond to more than changes in product design or packaging.

The second emphasis for reform in governance is *directional*, but directional in the sense of finding ways to reflect within the corporation the kinds of questioning and testing of answers that society is engaged in. In the absence of much clearer signals from society than we have or are likely to see, the directional goal should be to refocus private initiative so that it embraces a fuller range of society's concerns, but not to replace it with overly specific regulation.

These directional moves include questions about the basic charter of corporations. Should a federal standard replace a pattern of state rules and concessions? Should the proxy process be reformed to give more power to shareholders, or even to give voice to others with substantial interests who do not actually own stock? What can be done to make boards of directors less the mouthpiece of management and more effective as trustees for shareholders and for society as a whole? What changes are necessary within management itself, at all levels, in approaches to planning, operations, and control?

The third area for reform is *evaluative*. As cross-check on management, as feedback to them so that they can do their jobs better, and as feedback to society so that it will have a clearer idea of what it requires next, audits of corporate performance are likely to expand in thoroughness and scope. Currently the most specific changes are being considered for traditional financial audits, both by staffs within the firm and by outside accountants for public certification. Close behind, though, are initiatives for broader managerial and social audits, to begin the process of measuring systematically other than financial dimensions of performance.

Beyond these audits are the specialized supervisory and regulatory checks carried out by various agencies of government. These include cost reviews for defense contractors, monitoring of product quality and hiring practices, rulings on reserves and loan policies for banks, inspection for adherence to securities and antitrust laws, and thousands of other queries and controls. These have the potential for significant influence on governance if business knows that the collection of information will be followed by analysis, questioning, or some kind of federal intervention with corporate management.

The final area of reform in governance deals with *corrective* measures. The growth of the corporation and the problems of keeping it in line have outstripped the foundations of our legal system as much as they may have outstripped Adam Smith. It was convenient a hundred years ago to adopt the fiction that the corporation was a "person" and to apply the law according to that principle. However, as Christopher Stone has pointed out in a book called *Where the Law Ends*, such thinking is no longer sufficient.

Debate about governance includes a search for new kinds of economic and psychological incentives; for controls and penalties that are sufficiently specific to address current problems, yet flexible enough to fit future needs; for penalties that might try to improve organizational structure rather than simply punish companies for bad behavior; and for incentives and penalties that will sharpen the sense of personal responsibility among directors and managers.

Recent corrective reforms have placed a great deal of emphasis on separation of functions within boards of directors, between boards and management, and within managements to minimize potential for conflict of interest. The drive to minimize temptations, however, may be counterproductive in improving performance. Making corporations work better requires access to the best in ideas and experience, and the best is often going to come from people whose professional and business backgrounds are closely related to —not remote from—the business they are trying to advise. Access to competence risks involvement in conflict of interest, and challenges remain in finding ways to keep search for the one from being thwarted by fear of the other.

CRITERIA FOR PROGRESS IN GOVERNANCE

In asking how any eventual package of reforms should be judged, we can do worse than return to the thinking of John Maurice Clark in 1925. Clark wanted strongly to preserve the economic vigor and the private initiative which characterizes American business enterprise. Yet he did not believe that traditional economic rules of the game would stir business leaders to give enough attention to broader social issues. He examined various changes in "social control," many paralleling or leading toward what we are now examining as changes in "governance." His tests for a good system of control were these:

1. It must be democratic. This means that it must be exercised in the interests of the governed as they see their interests (not as some benevolent overlord might see them).
2. It should know what it wants. This sounds obvious and simple; but after what has been said as to how society acts, one can see that it presents some difficulties.
3. It must be powerful—powerful enough to make an unwilling minority obey the will of the majority. Incidentally, this means that

it must be searching enough to detect evasions and prompt enough to forestall violations so far as possible.

4. It must be efficient, and at the same time it must not destroy the efficiency of the thing it is regulating.

5. It must "economize coercion."

6. It must utilize all the strongest and most persistent motives of human nature, both generous and selfish: hope of reward, fear of punishment, and those loyalties, persuasions, and suggestions which have nothing directly to do with rewards and punishments, but which rest upon the deeper fact that the individual is essentially a part of the community.

7. The duties imposed must be simple enough to be understood; and this means, among other things, that social control must follow precedent a great deal of the time.

8. Control must be guided by experience or be wisely experimental.

9. It must be adaptable.

10. It must be farseeing. It must look beyond the immediate effect of doing a given thing to the further results of leading people to expect it in the future.

11. And, lastly, social control must be capable of progressively raising the level of mankind. In a democracy, where the mass of mankind does the ultimate controlling, this amounts to saying that social control must contrive, somehow, to rise higher than its source.

As we renew the search, these criteria are worth keeping in mind.

Lewis H. Young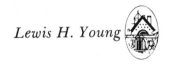

2

The Claimants
for Influence
with the Corporation

In the twenty years from 1948 to 1968, the U.S. economy turned in such a stellar performance that the U.S. corporation appeared to be performing its assigned role in the economic order in an exemplary way. The economy grew, on average 3.9 percent a year; the recovery from 1962 until 1968 was the longest in history, 28 million new jobs were created; corporate profits grew 102 percent, reaching a peak of $43 billion in the fourth quarter in 1968; and the stock market soared, with the Dow-Jones industrial average rising from 181 on January 2, 1948, to a closing of 945 on the night of December 30, 1968. During this period of solid economic growth, the American public generally approved of the performance and behavior of corporations. There was little criticism of the corporation or executives, except for a rare gripe from a stockholder that the dividend rate was too low (or an occasional loud and angry shout from students annoyed with the corporation, not for lack of performance, but for its war-related prosperity). But even these were few and far apart. Since the main object of stock investment for most investors in this period was appreciation of stock values, stock-

LEWIS H. YOUNG *is Editor-in-Chief of* Business Week, *with which he has been associated for more than a decade. He has also been writer and editor for* Electronics *and* Control Engineering.

holders encouraged companies' managements to pour profits back into the company rather than pay large dividends that the federal government would tax.

If a company did not perform well, as reflected in the movement and market price of the stock, the disappointed stockholder could —and would—sell the stock and, with the proceeds, seek out a better performer. There was little concern and little interest in how management made decisions, unless the decisions were reflected in the price of the stock. The ruling factors were the bottom line of the operating statement (profits after taxes) and the price of the stock.

As this golden period came to an end, circumstances changed. The go-go movement on Wall Street, after capturing the enthusiasm and money of a large number of shareholders, was running out of steam. Many of the acquisition-oriented conglomerates ran into trouble and the value of their stocks plummeted. Financial catastrophes began to hit corporations. The Penn Central, a $4 billion transportation and real estate company, went into bankruptcy, stunning the financial markets. When that failure collapsed the commercial paper markets, the Chrysler Corporation nearly followed suit. Wonder stocks such as National Student Marketing, ATO, and Litton Industries fizzled amid wide publicity. The collapse of stock prices in the early seventies tarnished the reputations of both corporations and corporate executives. Criticism was sounded that management was not running the business very well, and that managers were more concerned with their own compensation and stock options than they were in the health of the business.

When the Securities and Exchange Commission, in the seventies, began to discover evidence of corporate misconduct—illegal campaign contributions, questionable transactions, and bribes to foreign government officials, the tide ran against the corporation. As all these developments unfolded, public interest groups began to use the corporate machinery to achieve certain social goals: hiring of minorities and women, ending apartheid in Africa, speeding up the end of pollution.

By 1977 there was enough turmoil so that the SEC began hearings on corporate governance—who runs the corporation? The decade-old question of who controls the corporation—the stockholders or management—has been widened to include additional groups who believe they have some kind of claim on the behavior of a publicly-owned corporation.

Harold Williams, chairman of the SEC at this writing, prefers the term *corporate accountability* to describe the questions being asked about companies. The claimants for influence, in addition to stockholders who legally own the corporation, now include:

1. Employees—who are concerned about job security, compensation, health, and safety.
2. Customers, clients, and consumers—who expect the corporation to assume greater responsibility for the goods and services it offers, and how it offers them.
3. Public service groups—who want help in achieving social goals they have set.
4. Local governments—whose leaders worry about unemployment and its impact on elections.
5. Management, separated from ownership—which has established goals and aspirations that can differ sharply from other claimants for influence.

Because the list has grown so large and because he believes corporations are running out of control, Ralph Nader, the best known of the operators in the public service area, has proposed a series of tough restrictions on corporations to better control the behavior of companies. In his book *Taming the Giant Corporation*, Nader with his coauthors offers nine reasons why such drastic restrictions should be imposed:

1. The largest corporations have harmful market and nonmarket impacts.
2. State chartering laws, downgraded by the easy Delaware statutes, have failed to restrain corporate abuses.
3. The governing ethos of giant companies resembles an autocracy more than a democracy.
4. The officers of these corporations lack individual accountability for their actions.
5. Corporate secrecy has overwhelmed the needs for corporate disclosure.
6. Companies routinely violate the rights of their employees.
7. Widespread market concentration insulates most of our largest companies from the rigors of competition.
8. There has been an outbreak of corporate payoffs and other crimes.
9. Our chronic economic conditions amply demonstrate that these corporations are not performing well even by their own standards.

Few people outside Nader's own coterie would accept all nine of these statements as truth. For example, few companies *routinely* violate the rights of their employees as Nader claims; most people would credit government policy with having far more impact on economic conditions than the behavior of corporations. It is doubtful if the Congress would legislate the kind of corporate chartering of corporations that Nader envisions. If federal chartering does eventually happen, it is more likely to be far less restrictive; it could lay out general guidelines for behavior of corporations and require a certain number of outsiders on the board of directors. Part of the problem in achieving federal legislation is the diverse interests of the people who believe the corporation ought to be accountable. Many investors and executives believe no legislation is required; but if enough influential congressmen and senators think there is a problem with corporations, there will be legislation.

Shareholders

Legally, it is the shareholders that own the corporation. They elect directors who choose the management. And it is to the directors that management is accountable. According to the SEC, that system is breaking down; it doesn't work. The SEC staff asks some embarrassing questions that are hard for even corporate defenders to answer: Where are the checks and balances a corporation is supposed to have? Why don't directors oversee what management is doing? Why didn't directors protect the interest of shareholders? How were the directors answerable to the shareholders?

The answer to all these questions, according to Ralph Nader, is that shareholders have steadily been losing their rights and control for nearly a hundred years. The decline started in 1891 when New Jersey passed a Holding Company Act which authorized corporations to buy and sell stock or property of other corporations. Previously, a company was authorized to indulge only in a very narrow business set out in its charter. In 1896 New Jersey revised this act to allow corporations unlimited size; to reduce stockholder control by permitting classification of shareholders into preferred, common, and nonvoting groups; and to allow directors to amend the bylaws without stockholder consent. Then in 1899 Delaware passed the predecessor of its General Corporation Law and with the "most favorable of existing general corporation laws," determined to entice corporations into the state to raise local revenue. This first Delaware law reduced restrictions on corporations to a minimum.

Periodically, Delaware has revised its corporate laws to make the state an even more attractive home for companies. As an added aid, the Supreme Court of Delaware interprets the law to encourage a favorable business climate.

Although the SEC does not accept the Nader explanation completely, its staff does believe that such legislation, and the attitude of courts, has severely limited the ability of shareholders and investors to challenge management. In a number of recent cases that have reached the Supreme Court of the United States, such suits involving shareholders versus management have been referred back to state courts, where the judiciary tends to support management.

Because the SEC staff believes there is not much a shareholder can do, the SEC is pushing for new legislation that would give the shareholder legitimate claims in court. But such legislation has to be written very carefully lest it allow shareholders to interfere in the management of the company. The SEC wants to be sure that a shareholder who has been fraudulently disadvantaged by the management has a right to go into court. The relief is not for a shareholder to punish management for honest mistakes—that is the role of the stock market.

To the SEC there is growing shareholder dissatisfaction over corporate mismanagement that includes conflict of interest, unfair treatment of minority stockholders (particularly going private after taking the public's money at a much higher price per share), and the compensation and perquisites of management.

In framing legislation to help the shareholder, the SEC staff keeps coming back to the question: to whom is management responsible? As the SEC sees it, management selects the directors, and the shareholders have no real say in electing them. Of the 6,000 public corporations that file proxy materials with the SEC, the number of contested elections is minuscule. And in those contested elections, extremely rarely does management ever lose. There have even been a couple of corporations in which felons convicted of criminal charges were nominated as directors by management.

THE CHANGING SHAREHOLDER

During the past fifteen years, there has been a steady shift in stock ownership. Institutions such as mutual funds, pension funds, insurance companies, and bank trust departments have increased the share of corporations they own, while the percent owned by individuals has declined. The impact of the institutions has been greater in trading than in ownership. In 1978 institutional investors accounted for 70 percent of the dollar volume traded on the New York Stock Exchange each day (up from only 35 percent in 1963); but in a survey of 885 of the largest industrial and financial corporations, banks, and utilities in the December 26, 1977 issue of *Business Week*, the average ownership by institutions was only 22.4 percent of the outstanding shares. Institutional ownership ranged from a high of 60 percent at Amp Inc. and Consolidated Freightways to a low of zero at American Motors and Columbia Pictures.

Although the shift in ownership is clear and it is easy to see the impact institutional ownership has had on trading (it has increased volatility enormously), the impact on the governance of the corporation is arguable.

There have been a few cases where institutions have concerned themselves with material decisions the company has made. When Minneapolis' International Timesharing Corporation was having growing pains several years ago, a mutual fund and an insurance company, each with ownership of more than 10 percent of the stock, helped hire key people, acted as intelligence gatherers to obtain technological information on equipment, and helped find acquisition candidates.

As institutions buy and sell ever larger blocks of stock, they develop greater power in corporate affairs—power they occasionally exercise with the impact of a sledgehammer. But such exercises have been the exception rather than the rule. The rule was expressed by Frank J. Hoenemeyer, executive vice president of Prudential Life, in 1970: "We have been reluctant to use our economic power," he says. "As owners we abdicate responsibility every time we turn proxies over to management." Institutional stockholders have tended to vote proxies along the lines management of the corporation has recommended.

The truth is that what institutional owners are most interested in are major financings and acquisitions. Paul Hallingby, chairman of White Weld, a large investment banking firm, thinks there is more communication between investors and management than makes the press, but much of it has to do about the size of dividends or new issues. Hallingby says, "On cash dividends, institutional investors are vocal—not bashful."

In general, the important criteria for an institutional holder is

performance of the portfolio, because the first concern of fund shareholders is the value of their shares. A lot of institutions are less
investors than traders. Many of them will sell off a profitable stock
in a well-managed company to buy something the fund manager
believes is a bargain. It is not unusual for a mutual fund, for example, to replace 50 percent of its portfolio every year.

But if the institutions have rarely expressed their views on management subjects to the management, that attitude may be changing. Portfolio managers are on tenterhooks because the 1940 Investment Company Act does not spell out whether they should seek to
influence corporate managements or not. "We are perhaps at the
beginning of a trend," says Thomas R. Reeves, an executive with
Investors Diversified Services, the big mutual fund. "Increasingly we
have done less of the automatic voting of proxies." A prominent
Bostonian who heads a group of funds says:

> I'd like to do what brokers do—turn the shares over to their clients.
> But that is mechanically impossible. It's an awful responsibility. We
> had an experience recently where our vote decided whether a manage-
> ment stayed in or went out and it was terrible.

One fact that makes such an experience so terrible is the institutions' belief that they do not follow companies in a way that permits
them to vote the proxy. After the SEC completed its hearings on
corporate governance in 1977, Chairman Williams said he was
startled to learn that when a fund buys a stock recommended by
an analyst, that analyst never sees the proxy issued by the corporation; it goes somewhere else in the fund. Analysts told him, "We
don't look at a company that way. We don't know the company
well enough to express an opinion on how the proxy should be
voted."

Williams asked the rhetorical question, "If they don't, who does?
The general counsel?" Williams insisted that many analysts would
have a view on such matters as whether a specific compensation
plan for executives is merited, or whether staggered directorships
to avoid a takeover is reasonable, or whether to change the articles
of incorporation to require an 80 percent vote for a takeover is
reasonable—but they never express such views.

Williams believed that institutional ownership insulates management from the shareholder process. He said, "If you don't like the
company you sell your stock."

In Wall Street, people argue that that is the best way for institutions to influence management. Selling the stock in large blocks pushes the price of the stock down, increases the company's costs of raising capital, and punishes the management for poor performance. Sooner or later the management has to take into account the image the company has in the investor community, responding to that kind of subtle pressure to make decisions of which stockholders will approve.

At the SEC, the staff questions whether selling a stock is an adequate response for the small shareholder who has invested for the long term. If the price is pushed down far enough by the selling of institutional investors, the small investor cannot afford to sell at such a loss, or there may not be a market for the stock when the institutions finish. (On September 29, 1972 the price of the stock of Levitz Furniture Company fell nearly 30 percent, from forty-seven dollars to thirty-three dollars a share, in thirty minutes as many institutions dumped the stock. Later that same year, the stock of Handelman Company lost 51 percent of its value in a single trade by an institution.) In an extreme case, the price of the stock falls so low the management can use corporate funds to buy up the outstanding shares and turn the corporation into a privately-owned company. Or if there are one or only a very few large stockholders, the small investor can be treated unfairly when the stock has been depressed by institutional selling pressure.

In the expansionist days of the sixties, most companies eagerly sought big institutional investors to buy their stock. The commonly held belief was that these sophisticated, well-informed investors would buy up a company's stock and that would mean stability. But it has not worked out that way. Because institutional investors can sell suddenly and erratically and because they tend to follow a few of the very biggest and best-named (like the Morgan Guaranty Bank), many companies now prefer smaller individual stockholders whose ownership is widely distributed. Not only does this make for greater price stability, but with wide stock ownership an outsider finds it far more difficult to gain control of the company. A clear example of the kind of threat institutional ownership can be to a corporation is the case of Becton Dickinson, the drug and medical equipment producer. In February 1978, Sun Oil was able to buy 34 percent—and control—of it by purchasing stock from fewer than forty owners, most of them institutions.

Designing remedies for shareholders, the SEC seems to be seeking help primarily for the individual investor. Its staff believes that the big institutions have the legal clout to take care of themselves. But planning remedies is complicated by the differing goals of stockholders. Many are interested in holding a stock only for a short period of time. This is particularly true of institutional investors. But unless a shareholder holds a stock for a very long time, he cannot work on the management to help shape its policy. Institutions defend their behavior on the grounds that their job is to maximize the return on investment, not to force management of the corporation to behave in any particular way.

But even many small investors will hold a stock only until they believe its market value has peaked or a broker advises them to sell. Those who hold stocks for a long time tend to fall into the "widows and orphans" category and often do not know enough about the details of operations of the corporations whose stock they own to try to influence management.

At the SEC, the staff insisted that its hearings on corporate governance were aimed at restoring confidence in the markets. The staff blamed some of the cause of the steady decline in stock prices in the 1974 to 1978 period on a lack of confidence by investors. If current trends continue, however, there will be fewer and fewer small investors interested in buying shares of companies. More and more alternative investments are being offered, from municipal bonds to commodities to options. Unless most institutional investors change their organization and method of operation, they will not have either the capability or interest to hold accountable for anything but good financial performance the managements of companies in which the investor holds stock.

Employees

After World War II Britain's Labor Party, then in power, imposed a system of forced participation management of corporations in conquered West Germany. Under this system, called codetermination *(Mitbestimmung)*, the supervisory board of directors was composed of representatives of shareholders (two-thirds) and representatives of the workers (one-third), except in the steel and coal industry where the representation was split fifty-fifty, with a public representative to break tie votes. In a German company the supervisory board elects the top management and passes on major decisions of the company such as the level of wage increases to be granted and major investment plans.

In January 1976, an effort by the Social Democratic government of Helmar Schmidt to increase labor's participation so it would control the supervisory board was defeated. Even so, codetermination was extended so that a supervisory board is now composed of six shareholder representatives, six labor representatives, and a chairman elected by the representatives of the shareholders. One of the labor representatives must be an employee elected by upper-middle management, effectively guaranteeing shareholder control of the corporation.

Efforts to spread codetermination elsewhere have had mixed results. In Sweden in 1976, the *Riksdag* (parliament) passed the Law on Codetermination in Working Life, thus mandating worker participation in the management of Swedish companies and multinational companies operating in Sweden. So far the practical details of how to make the system function have been left to individual companies, many of whom had instituted codetermination mechanisms voluntarily before the law was passed. An effort to impose codetermination on other members of the European Economic Community failed because nobody, except for a few European labor leaders, really wants it.

Management certainly does not. Executives see codetermination as an impediment to efficient running of the organization. They fear they would have to depend on union support for their jobs. The horrible example raised in Germany is the dismissal in 1975 of Rudolf Leiding as chairman of Volkswagen. Leiding, admittedly abrasive with unionists, was forced to resign by the supervisory board when members of the political party in power (the SPD) on the board, representing the government's 40 percent ownership in the company, voted with workers. The key issue was Leiding's proposal to build a Volkswagen plant in the United States.

But the Leiding incident has been the exception in companies where codetermination has been employed. In twenty-four years of operation at the chemical giant Farbwerke Hoechst, the worker representatives on the supervisory board have never voted against management. Still, codetermination remains a controversial issue among managers and workers. One of the worker representatives on the board explained, "It is hard to make our work understandable to workers here. The mass of voters and workers have never fully recognized the value of codetermination."

On the other hand, many West German executives credit codetermination for Germany's record of relatively few strikes and very large gains in productivity. Interestingly, in 1973, when West Germany had one of its rare bouts of serious labor trouble, the longest and most violent strikes occurred at the steel and coal companies that already had 50 percent worker participation on the supervisory boards. Many of these worker representatives had been coopted. They were able to see management's problems so clearly they lost touch with the rank and file of the unions.

Many German executives believe that if the object of codetermination is to bring the worker into a position where he feels involved in the company and the business, there are better ways of accomplishing involvement. They suggest forms of profit sharing or employee stock ownership. The German Employers Association pushed worker acquisition of company ownership as a means of heading off higher wage demands in 1978.

Outside Germany and Sweden, the concept of codetermination has not won widespread acceptance. In England, even though a government study (The Bullock Report) recommended legislating some form of worker participation, the Callaghan government shelved the proposal in 1977 because representatives of both labor and management had serious qualms about it. Executives at Imperial Chemical Industries, Britain's biggest chemical company, found that workers did not want to be involved in broad corporate decision-making, such as where to make investments and what kinds of technology to employ. What the workers really wanted was a bigger say in how their individual jobs were structured and on working conditions.

In France the Suddreau Plan, the French approach to codetermination that once was part of President Valery Giscard d'Estaing's program for "the advanced liberal society," has been shoved aside by the argument over economic policy in France. It was easy to sidetrack because labor opposition to the concept was particularly keen. Communist and socialist unions in France see nationalization of industry as the best way to achieve worker participation in industry. Even if the country is to have privately-owned companies, these unions want no part of cooperation with management. Explains Michel Rolant, economic counselor of the Socialiste Confédération Française Démocratique du Travail: "French unions are not German unions. We believe in keeping some distance between management and labor. Codetermination with management is not what we are striving for."

That kind of reaction is why even many who believe codetermination has been a positive and effective force in West Germany are not sure it can be exported to other countries. German workers tend to be more disciplined; German unions tend to be docile; German union leaders factor in the role German exports play in the economy when they design their demands on industry to make sure they do not price German goods out of world markets. In addition, the Social Democrats have legislated into being many of the measures demanded by labor: increased health and unemployment insurance, improved on-the-job medical care, strengthened protection against unjust firings, and increased power for local unions.

In the United States, labor union leaders have always opposed their participation in management on philosophical grounds. In general, the goal of union leaders has been to extract as much in the way of benefits and pay from the company as possible. Being part of management, they believe, would interfere with this objective.

American workers, like those of Imperial Chemical, are more interested in how their jobs are structured, working conditions, and pay than in broad corporate strategy. The one exception is job security. The growth of conglomerate-type companies that acquire and merge other companies—sometimes reducing work forces, moving operations to other locations, or shutting down plants—has prompted many workers to want a veto on corporate plans that cause large-scale layoffs. Both the united autoworkers and the steelworkers have proposed some form of the lifetime employment that is enjoyed by many Japanese workers.

But if workers are not interested in sharing in the major decisions the corporation makes, they are going to demand greater participation in decision-making that affects health and safety. The long-term objective could be to model a procedure after the system that has been adopted in Sweden. There each plant has one worker designated as an environmental watchdog. That worker has the authority to shut down the plant if he believes working conditions have deteriorated to the point where they endanger employees' health. To some union people this idea is more attractive than a government agency, like the Occupational Safety and Health Administration (OSHA), because such a system leads to immediate action. Action by a government agency, on the other hand, can take months or years before implementation.

Consumers

Ralph Nader has become the symbol of an outside force making the corporation accountable to its customers. His approach has been to file legal actions against corporations he feels violate consumers' rights and to prepare, publish, and widely publicize reports about products and companies. Nader's newest thrust is a demand for federal chartering of corporations. Although others have talked about federal charters, too, Nader has advocated the most extreme approach.

With federal chartering enacted, Nader believes executives would not be able to make the kind of decisions that have led to "irresponsible technology, product dangers, pollution, and monopoly practices." Nader's law would, for example, require companies to substantiate the claims in all advertisements, grant consumers expanded rights in class action suits, force companies that dominate markets to divest themselves of assets, and prohibit a company from acquiring any of the largest eight corporations in any industry. Nader would make the corporation accountable to the consumer through law.

But there is another, softer, approach which has been espoused by consumerists such as Esther Peterson, a consultant on consumer affairs to President Carter. Peterson is not so sure that legislation is the route to follow. She fears that statutes and regulation will keep companies who want to be responsive to consumers from introducing new measures. She fears that "we are so stifled with regulation we are killing innovation. People who want to change are afraid to change because of laws and regulations." All Peterson would do with law is set the principle that corporations are accountable to the public.

Because she believes a new kind of consciousness is being built into corporations, she believes that change should be structured into the company by the company. She would have consumer-minded people in the policy-making power structure. She says, "I would rather see a consumer representative in the operating end of the company, where the day-to-day action takes place, than on the board." But she would backstop that with members of the board of directors who are public-minded, people who have the consumer in mind.

The crux of the consumer's concern is found in three sets of questions:

1. Are products being manufactured of good quality; are they designed to become obsolete too quickly or to wear out too easily?
2. Are corporations satisfying the real needs of their customers? Or are they making products and services that are unhealthy and wasteful?
3. Are corporations supplying real information about their products and services and what they will do?

To answer such questions requires wisdom beyond the reach of either government agencies and bureaucrats or corporate executives. But consumerists keep asking questions such as: "Do consumers need sugared cereals? Do consumers need potato chips in tennis ball cans? Do consumers need shampoo that is apricot-scented?"

Peterson admits that it is hard, if not impossible, to answer such questions. But she insists the line can be drawn around areas of real danger. She says, "A company can't put a product on the market if it knows it is going to cause cancer or hurt the environment." And she adds, "If a product might be dangerous, like cigarettes, let people know." These kinds of consumerists are prepared to let customers make such decisions for themselves *if* the corporation producing the product properly discloses the potential danger to the customer.

Consumerists believe the idea that customers can protest corporate behavior by not buying products is naive—"a lovely idea, but it isn't true." Most consumers, it is charged, do not have sufficient information to make a good choice because technology is so complicated or because monopolistic conditions so restrict the choice that none can be made. Thus, the effort to make the corporation accountable to consumers continues to grow.

Public Interest Groups

In February 1970, the Project for Corporate Responsibility, a small nonprofit group in Washington, D.C., launched an attack to make General Motors "responsible" by changing the corporation's life style and values. The program was named Campaign GM. The group bought twelve shares (of the 287.5 million then outstanding) so it had the right to bring its proposals to a stockholders vote by way of the corporate proxy statement. The group started out with three demands:

1. Amend the certificate of incorporation to put GM on record as limiting its business purposes to those consistent with public's health and safety.
2. Expand the board of directors from twenty-four to twenty-seven members to make room for three representatives of public interest.
3. Require management to set up a shareholders' committee to police the public impact of GM decisions and determine its proper role in society.

Barely were these demands sent to the corporation when Campaign GM added six more issues pertaining to car-crash resistance, vehicle emissions, warranty provisions, pollution from manufacturing plants, support for public transportation, and opportunities for black employment.

None of these demands was ever approved by stockholders despite a bitterly contested battle between GM's management and the Project for Corporate Responsibility. In fact, they were all voted down. But as an aftermath to the bitter struggle, GM did amend its corporate pose. In the past three years particularly, it has adopted a position of working with regulators to achieve better emission control through the catalytic muffler and improved collision resistance with the air bag. It added outside environmental and personnel experts. And it elected a well-known black, Dr. Leon Sullivan, to the board of directors.

The Project for Corporate Responsibility made a major impact on General Motors. Even more importantly, it showed other groups, groups who want the corporation to influence public policy in a variety of matters, that the corporation is subject to pressure and will respond to it.

From this model have come such diverse activities as antiwar demonstrations at stockholder meetings of companies, like Honeywell and Dow, which supplied military material; opposition to Portuguese colonialism in Angola by the Presbyterian Church at Gulf Oil stockholder meetings; criticism of doing business in South Africa at annual meetings of many companies, including Polaroid and IBM.

Sometimes these groups have purchased a small number of company shares of stock, in the pattern of Campaign GM. But more often they have tried to impose their influence through other shareholders. In its struggle against Gulf, the Presbyterian Church tried to persuade Presbyterian stockholders to vote against the company. At Stanford University in 1977, students demonstrated on campus to force the university administration to clean out of its endowment fund any stock in a company that did business with South Africa.

To date, most individual and institutional stockholders have ignored such pressures. The exceptions have been a few eleemosynary institutions where there is great social presence on the board level. A few universities have given in to student pressures, and the administrators of trust funds have managed portfolios in response. A few teachers' pension funds, too, have selected their portfolio with an eye to achieving good social conscience as much as to earning a good return. But the threat of penalties for imprudent management, imposed by the Employees Retirement Insurance and Security Act (ERISA), keeps most fund managers from relying on social conscience to make investment decisions.

Still, there is likely to be more such pressure on corporations. Because of the multinational nature of the modern company, it is ubiquitous in its operations. That universality makes it attractive as a means to influence a wide variety of public policies. A good segment of the populace attributes to the corporation far more power and clout than the corporation can really exert. It is a popular fiction that corporations can make or break governments, can change legislation at will, and can force consumers to buy any quantity of any product. The first two beliefs may have been true years ago, but they are not true today. Even weak countries like Zaire and Angola can dictate exactly what companies that operate within their borders can and cannot do. And these countries hold the threat of nationalization over the multinational companies like a perpetual sword of Damocles; many of these countries wield the sword too. Regulators and legislators are very careful and very correct in their contact with industry representatives. Some will not even meet with someone from industry unless some third party is present.

Management

The separation of ownership from management has, as might be expected, resulted in these two groups having different goals and objectives. The stockholder is interested primarily in achieving a satisfactory return on his investment or conserving his assets or gaining appreciation of the value of the stock or several of these. Management is primarily concerned with personal compensation, career growth, job security, appreciation of stock prices to make options valuable, or all or some of these. As the management owns a smaller and smaller share of the corporation, its interests diverge from the shareholder even more widely.

Management, it is often charged, runs the corporation for its benefit rather than for the stockholders'. The staff at the SEC argues that "the corporate treasury does not belong to management, but the management has unlimited access to it for the purpose of entrenching itself." In the book *The Industrial State,* John Kenneth Galbraith charges that many of the steps corporations take are for the benefit of the technocracy: acquiring companies to provide advancement for management, for example. Ralph Nader in the *Taming of the Giant Corporation* claims:

> The common theme of these many instances of mismanagement is a failure to restrain the power of senior executives. A corporate chief executive's decision to expand, merge, or even violate the law can often be made without accountability to outside society.

Whether this view is accurate or not, it has influenced the thinking of the SEC and many of the staff members of the agency subscribe to it. At the SEC a lot of effort is being expended to answer the question: for whose benefit is the corporation being run?

Harold Williams has stated that the system of the stock price penalizing bad management is in danger of breaking down.

> The management of an individual company can say "All right, the stock is going to sell at fourteen dollars rather than thirty-five dollars a share. That's fine if I can be sure nobody is going to take me over and I can get my salary to run the company the way I want. That's all I want."

To prevent takeovers in such circumstances, some managements have changed the articles of incorporation so that 80 percent of the stockholders must approve a takeover, or terms of directors are staggered so that only one-third are elected every year. In addition, thirty-three states have passed laws prohibiting corporate takeovers or making them difficult to complete, thus making management harder to remove. Since takeovers often allow the shareholder to obtain a price for his stock that is well over the market price, such restrictive acts are often not in his interest.

Part of the public's suspicion of business is reflected in a growing demand that all the compensation—including fringe benefits and perquisites—of management be disclosed widely. The SEC staff claims that nobody is upset by a corporate aircraft or a corporate apartment for a top executive as long as it is disclosed. But, the staff charges, "Hundreds of thousands of dollars of corporate money are going into the pockets of managers, and shareholders do not know about it."

As the SEC waged war against failure to disclose perquisites (perks) in 1978, these rewards were becoming less of a real issue among executives. The reason is that as corporations disclosed perks, the Internal Revenue Service moved aggressively to tax them as income. Since most executives were already in brackets whose marginal income is taxed well in excess of 50 percent, the perks had become very expensive. Included in the list that IRS deems as income are company-paid cars, seats on corporate jet aircraft, hotel suites, club memberships, low-interest loans, and personal financial counseling.

In the United States perks never achieved the same pervasiveness they did in Europe. Because of the excessively high tax rates on the continent, few corporate executives want high salaries. In 1977, for example, the chairman of Barclays, Britain's biggest bank, earned only $31,000 after taxes—not as much as most middle-level managers in an average American corporation. But in Europe it is not unusual for an executive to have his car, home, vacation home, household help, and entertainment paid for by the company.

Despite the government crack down on perks in 1977, some of them clearly improve corporate efficiency. For example, the degradation of commercial jet aircraft schedules since the oil crunch of 1974 has often made executive travel time-consuming and inconvenient. There are many cities that cannot be visited on a one-day trip by commercial jet aircraft. Too often it has become impossible to get a reservation for last minute trips. The only way an executive can make these kinds of forays is by private plane. Similarly, chauffeur driven cars—with the chauffeur doubling as a security guard—make a lot of sense in a world that is increasingly subject to terrorist tactics that include kidnapping, murder, and threats of bodily harm against corporate executives because they are executives. The IRS has never exhibited much concern about productivity, its own or anyone else's. Its efforts to tax perks and fringe benefits—including even subsidized meals in company cafeterias—

reflect an agency running out of rational control rather than a philosophy being applied.

In general, the public believes that corporate executives are highly paid, and probably overpaid. But, in fact, corporate executives who are responsible for enterprises that employ tens of thousands of people do not receive compensation equivalent to the great responsibility they have or to the gigantic salaries earned by entertainers and sports figures. When the progressivity of the federal income tax is added to state and local income taxes, the high rate of inflation, and the demise of so many tax shelters, the average executive is not so well paid today as his counterpart was twenty years ago or even ten years ago.

Because of the size and complexity of so many corporations, only the management, which is close to day-to-day activities, can know and understand the details of operations. Directors cannot and stockholders cannot. Thus it is hard to see how the government can curb management without seriously interfering with the corporation's operations and efficiency. New legislation to ban illegal acts is not necessary; such behavior is already against the law. The problem seems to be in enforcement. The SEC says it does not have the staff to investigate every case of misconduct by corporate management, and the state courts are often reluctant to interfere with corporate operations.

The best answer that has surfaced is to put more pressure on the independent auditors and the board of directors to hold them responsible for curbing the excesses of management.

Threat of Tomorrow

Today only a small but very vocal group is calling for reform in corporate governance. But the trend of opinion in America is clearly toward being increasingly distrustful of business. Rightly or wrongly, the public believes that business is self-centered, motivated by its own profit, and interested in what it can get away with. There is not a large articulate supportive group for the corporate system, even though it has brought about the highest standard of living in the world. That is why people who have studied the problem, like Harold Williams, predict that the group will get bigger. He adds:

> It all goes back to a growing sense that the American corporation is
> irresponsible, does whatever it can get away with; and we have to stop

it. The next time we have a corporate disaster, it will be a larger group of people. . . . There is a lot of latent support out there.

Part of this support stems from the growing attractiveness of egalitarianism, a movement that seeks greater equality of condition—more equal distribution of income, housing, consumer goods, and social status. Egalitarians believe that the great corporations already have wrecked the private enterprise system. They see the corporation as a villain that must be restrained by massive government intervention. An article in *Business Week* described their view this way:

> They blame big business for cheating the poor and rewarding the rich. They see the corporation as a nameless, faceless, menacing manipulator of their lives. They resent the hierarchical structure of management, the payment of big salaries and bonuses to top executives, and the flow of dividends to stockholders. They blame corporations for high prices, for air and water pollution, and for depleting natural resources. Most of all, they blame corporations for not using their economic power to impose equality on their employees.

Egalitarians make their claims for economic benefits in terms of rights. They are not likely to win them all overnight. But the United States is in for a slow shift toward more equal incomes. And the corporation, as the dynamo of the economy, will be in the middle of the shift.

Consumerist Esther Peterson has another way of putting it. She says, "We are living in a stage in history where all the people who are out want in." Applied to the corporation, that means that groups that never had any association with corporations now believe they have a claim on influencing business.

Elliott J. Weiss

3

Governance, Disclosure, and Corporate Legitimacy

Introduction

"Sunlight is the best disinfectant, electric light the best policeman." This statement, made by Louis D. Brandeis in 1916, has come to epitomize one of the central themes of the system by which large corporations are governed in the United States—that corporate decision-making be regulated through mandatory disclosure requirements rather than direct government intervention. Some commentators, in fact, have suggested that disclosure could provide something close to a universal cure to the ills associated with the activities of large, publicly-held corporations. Consequently, at a time when public concern about corporations is proliferating, it should not be surprising that expanding the scope of corporate disclosure requirements is discussed.

Yet Brandeis' aphorism raises at least as many questions as it

ELLIOTT J. WEISS *is Associate Professor at the Benjamin N. Cardozo School of Law, Yeshiva University. Professor Weiss was Executive Director of the Investor Responsibility Research Center (1972–76) and Writer-in-Residence of The Conservation Foundation (1976–77). A member of The Advisory Committee on Corporate Disclosure of the SEC (1976–77), he has written widely on business problems.*

answers. Is sunlight always the best disinfectant, or is its efficacy dependent on other elements? If the latter, what elements render sunlight—disclosure, that is—most effective? What kinds of corporate conduct, if any, are not likely to be influenced by disclosure? In considering the potential of disclosure as a response to emerging concerns about the governance and activities of large, publicly-held corporations, these questions must be answered.

The process of developing answers should begin with a description and evaluation of the American system of corporate governance—that is, the system used to select the people who control corporations and to regulate their activities—and the role disclosure plays in that system. That will be our first subject. Then, the contribution that new disclosure requirements might make to dealing with defects in the corporate governance system will be considered.

The Market and the Governance System

If corporations operated in a perfectly efficient market, and if the market took account of all of society's interest in any transaction, questions about corporate governance would be of no more than trivial importance to society. A perfectly efficient market would react surely and swiftly on the basis of accurate and comprehensive information. It would provide those in control of corporations with signals indicating the only course of action consistent with profitability. Corporate managers who read those signals correctly would retain their positions of control; but, because profit margins would be razor-thin, firms whose managers misread the market's signals would rapidly become bankrupt. The swiftness, accuracy, and decisiveness of the market's judgments would render unimportant how the managers had been selected in the first place.

However, the market in which corporations—and particularly the large, publicly-held corporations that are the subject of this work—operate is far from perfectly efficient. Carl Kaysen, writing in 1959, stated that "typically, the large corporation . . . operates in a situation where the constraints imposed by market forces are loose, and the scope for managerial choice is considerable." Many industries, Kaysen noted, are dominated by a few firms that have substantial market power and that are at least partially insulated from competitive pressures. In all industries, many decisions are made to which the market's reaction is discernible only after the passage of a substantial time period. These factors, Kaysen said, allow corporate managers substantial discretion in such important areas as "prices and price-cost relations, investment, location, research and innovation, and product character and selling effort." ("The Corporation: How Much Power? What Scope?" in Edward S. Mason [ed.] *The Corporation in Modern Society.*)

The intensity of competition in most major industries has not changed materially since 1959, nor have delays in market judgments become less important. Managers of large corporations still decide whether to raise or lower prices when their factories are operating at well below full capacity, whether new plants should be built in the "New South" or old ones should be refurbished in New England, what levels and kinds of research and development activities they should support, and whether they are sufficiently confident about the government's economic policies to commit their companies to major new investment programs. In short, imperfections in the market allow managers a great deal of discretion in the use of corporations' resources. Since corporate managers control a major position of American society's productive resources, the fact that they have substantial discretion means they also possess substantial power. It matters greatly how these managers are selected and controlled.

Other kinds of imperfections in the market have amplified the importance to society of the process through which corporations are governed. The 1960s and 1970s might well be called the Age of Externalities—a period during which the American public became acutely aware that even a perfect competitive market does not take account of negative externalities such as pollution and urban blight, or positive externalities such as job satisfaction and esthetic pleasure. An exclusively economic orientation, it was recognized, allowed managers to escape being accountable for the social impact of their decisions.

The growth in public awareness about "externalities" led affected groups to initiate a variety of efforts to reduce managers' discretions, particularly their discretion to increase social costs. Many federal and state regulatory statutes were passed; and regulatory agencies were created to deal with problems created in the large part by corporate activities such as environmental pollution, lack of equal employment opportunity, occupational health and safety hazards, consumer frauds, and unsafe products.

Over time, though, it became clear to most observers that these regulatory efforts could achieve no more than limited success. Some of the problems with regulation lay in the difficulties that government had in formulating and implementing well-designed regulatory strategies. Some lay in the way that certain regulatory strategies hindered market efficiency. But often programs failed, at least in part, as a result of the efforts of corporation managers to prevent enactment of really effective legislation or of strong implementation measures. Often, too, it seemed that programs were frustrated by massive corporate resistance to the efforts of government agencies to enforce their regulatory requirements. Such experience highlighted for many people both the power held by corporate managers and the social importance of limiting that power.

In sum, defects in the market and in government regulatory programs create a situation in which those in control of large corporations—the dominant nongovernmental institutions in American society—possess great discretionary power in the way they use the resources they command. Consequently, how those persons are selected and how they are controlled are matters of enormous importance to society.

The Corporate Governance System: The Model

A major purpose of the corporate governance system is to provide legitimacy to those who manage corporations. Kenneth Boulding has observed:

> Large organized social systems . . . always require legitimacy. . . . If an institution or organization loses legitimacy, it may operate for a while in the underground, but the probability of its survival is severely reduced.

("The Dynamics of Legitimacy," in Neil Jacoby [ed.] *The Business-Government Relationship: A Reassessment.*) This statement appears applicable to corporate managers. American society is not likely to allow them to remain in their positions unless they can be shown to be accountable for their use of power.

Yet legitimacy cannot be defined or measured easily, nor can it be obtained directly. Rather, like happiness, it is a by-product of other activities. Since corporate managers obtain only a limited amount of legitimacy from the operations of the market and of government regulations, they must also draw legitimacy from the way they are selected and monitored from outside.

The corporate governance system has four major elements: a corporate electoral process, the stock market, state corporate law, and disclosure requirements promulgated under the federal securities laws. We shall examine here how, in a conceptual sense, these four elements should operate to regulate the behavior of corporate managers and assure their accountability. In the section that follows, we shall consider how the governance system actually operates.

THE ELECTORAL PROCESS

Corporations are governed through a system commonly described as democratic. An electoral mechanism—the election of directors by shareholders at an annual meeting—lies at the heart of the system. Directors are charged with managing or overseeing the management of a corporation's business. They are made accountable to the shareholders by requirements that directors regularly stand for election.

Three assumptions underlie the electoral system. One is that shareholders wish corporations to operate as profitably as possible. The second is that shareholders can and will make informed judgments about whether directors have used their power to maximize profits. The third is that shareholders will replace directors who have not used their power to maximize profits with persons who will use that power. If these assumptions are correct, shareholders' judgment will compensate for weaknesses in the market's judgments, and the electoral process will ensure selection of directors who will use their power efficiently. By dint of being elected, these directors will be considered legitimate.

THE STOCK MARKET

The existence of a market for corporate stock is supposed to enhance the effectiveness of the corporate electoral process. The governance system model assumes that if a corporation's shareholders do not elect directors who use their power efficiently, the corporation will be managed poorly and will fare poorly in the marketplace. As a consequence, the price of the company's stock will decline. People who are not shareholders will recognize the opportunity provided by this situation, purchase a controlling interest in the corporation, and then use the voting power they have acquired to elect more competent directors. Thus, just as shareholders' power is supposed to serve as a safeguard against directors' inefficient use of corporate power, stock market power is supposed to serve as a safeguard against shareholders' inefficient use of electoral power.

CORPORATE LAW

Certain aspects of corporate law support or supplement the other parts of the governance system. Perhaps most importantly, corporate law establishes the ground rules for the corporate electoral process. Under the laws of most states, at least one-third of a corporation's board must stand for election each year, and no director can be elected for a term longer than three years. Corporate law also requires that shareholder meetings be held at least annually and establishes procedures through which shareholders can call special meetings to remove directors. These legal requirements also preserve the market for corporate control by preventing corporate managements from taking action to insulate themselves from shifts in stock ownership and voting control.

Corporate law also imposes certain fiduciary obligations on corporate directors and gives every shareholder in a corporation the right to sue if a director's performance does not meet those obligations. Directors' obligations can be classified crudely as a duty of loyalty to the corporation and a duty to exercise due care in the use of their power. The first is intended to assure that a director will use his power over corporate resources to serve corporate purposes rather than personal interests. The second is meant to assure that a director will use reasonable care in making discretionary decisions. The goal, again, is to promote corporations' competitive efficiency.

The legal system supplements the electoral process and the market for control, in a conceptual sense, by allowing a single shareholder to remedy inefficiency that has not been recognized by either the majority of shareholder-electors or by the stock market. It also allows a corporation to recoup from a director losses due to his inefficient or self-serving use of corporate power, a result that cannot be attained through the electoral process. Finally, the legal system is supposed to protect minority shareholders from attempts by majority shareholders or their agents to use corporate resources to promote the interests of the majority where they conflict with the interests of the corporation.

THE DISCLOSURE SYSTEM

Clearly, without adequate information about directors' use of corporate power,

1. shareholders would not know whether directors should be removed or reelected;
2. persons who were not shareholders would find it difficult to decide whether to attempt to purchase control of a corporation; and
3. shareholders would be hard put to determine on a timely basis when directors or majority shareholders had taken actions that violated their fiduciary obligations.

To deal with weaknesses in the governance of large, publicly-held corporations resulting from lack of information, Congress passed the Securities Exchange Act of 1934. The 1934 Act implicitly endorsed the basic elements of the corporate governance system established by state laws and set out to ensure that sufficient information was available to allow the system to function properly. The Act focused on the corporate electoral process and delegated to the Securities and Exchange Commission authority to require corporations to disclose all information "necessary or appropriate . . . to ensure the fairness of the proxy solicitation process." With this authority, the SEC could require publicly-held corporations to distribute information about candidates for election as their directors, about the company's business activities (including detailed periodic financial reports), about directors' decisions, and about transactions where a director's interests and those of the corporation were potentially in conflict. It was thought that by ensuring the availability of this information, efficient functioning of the corporate governance system could be ensured. The knowledge that transactions would have to be disclosed was supposed to influence corporate managers to use their power prudently and properly. Where disclosure did not deter unwise or improper use of managers' power, the electoral process, the stock market, or corporate law could be expected to remedy the situation.

The Corporate Governance System: The Reality

The disclosure system, as administered by the SEC, has facilitated the operation of the mechanisms of the corporate governance system and also has effectively policed a wide variety of corporate transactions. Still, it has not eliminated major discrepancies between how the system is supposed to function and how it actually works. The disclosure system also has largely failed to address what many observers believe is a major conceptual flaw in the governance system—that it does not take explicit account of values other than competitive efficiency. Largely as a result of these problems in concept and operation of the system of corporate governance, the legitimacy of those who hold positions of power in large companies has become a subject of debate.

The essence of this controversy is expressed in the following trenchant observation by Edward S. Mason in *The Corporation in Modern Society*:

> But by now we are all aware that we live not only in a corporate society but a society of large corporations. The management—that is, the control—of these corporations is in the hands of, at most, a few thousand men. Who selected these men, if not to rule over us, at least to exercise vast authority, and to whom are they responsible? The answer to the first question is quite clearly: they selected themselves. The answer to the second is, at best, nebulous. This, in a nutshell, constitutes the problem of legitimacy.

Since 1959, when Mason made this statement, the problem has become appreciably more serious.

THE ELECTORAL PROCESS

In most corporations the electoral process is virtually meaningless. The chief executive officer usually dominates the process, selecting candidates for election to the board who, recommended by management, are virtually assured of election. By and large, these directors are either other senior executives of the corporation or persons from outside friendly to management. In most cases they will neither make major decisions nor serve as stern taskmasters. Rather, they will act as sympathetic advisers and will move to oust ineffective executives only when, to use the words of one astute observer of corporate boards, "even the manager's own mother would have long since gotten rid of him."

The Economics of the Process—The corporate electoral process languishes because shareholders are apathetic, and their apathy is due in large part to the unattractive economics of shareholder activism. The costs of challenging managements' candidates are very high, particularly when viewed in relation to the size of all but the largest shareholders' economic interests in the corporation. It probably would require several hundred thousand dollars to elect non-management directors in a large corporation or even to defeat one management nominee. To succeed, a dissident shareholder would have to marshal information demonstrating inadequacies in directors' performance. Then, armed with that information, he would have to publish independently material soliciting the support of other shareholders, clear it through the SEC, and distribute it to the other shareholders. Under state corporate laws and the SEC's proxy rules, the corporation would not be required to circulate his materials or to assist him by doing more than making available names and addresses of other shareholders. Moreover, incumbent management has a relatively free hand to use corporate resources to combat a dissident's campaign. Thus, ousting a management fighting to retain its control of a corporation is a difficult and expensive task.

Having risked substantial sums, a dissident cannot recover his expenses if he loses and is not assured of reimbursement if he succeeds. Unless a dissident wins an attractive management position as a result of his efforts, he will realize no more than modest financial benefits from ousting incompetent or ineffective directors. The benefits will flow to all shareholders in proportion to their interests in the corporation. Thus, while the total benefits flowing from a dissident's action may far outweigh the costs of a successful challenge, for most individual shareholders, challenging management through the electoral process is not economically appealing.

Occasionally, to be sure, proxy fights for corporate control are initiated; but most such efforts bear little obvious relationship to theories of corporate efficiency. Rather, they involve hoopla-filled campaigns by rival groups, both often more interested in what the corporation can do for them than in what they can do for the corporation.

Electoral challenges by shareholders could be expected to occur with some frequency if shareholders were locked into their investments in corporations for extended periods of time. This is true even though, as has been restated ad nauseum, the average shareholder is more interested in dividends and the possibility of capital gains than in managing a company or selecting its managers. Locked-in shareholders would have greater incentives to challenge inefficient managements.

However, dissatisfied shareholders are not locked in. They need not vote with their proxies because they can "vote with their feet" —sell their stock—at almost any time simply by telephoning their stockbrokers.

The Importance of Exit—The significance of this alternative is highlighted by the work of Albert O. Hirschman, an economist. In *Exit, Voice and Loyalty,* Hirschman begins with the premise that all large organizations are subject to a basic entropic force—a "loss of optimizing aptitude or energy"—which causes them to operate at less than peak efficiency, and that two approaches are available to reduce the slack that results from this trend. Hirschman terms one "exit": people sever their connection with the organization as a consequence of dissatisfaction with the quality of what it is producing for them. He calls the other "voice": people remain within the organization and attempt to remedy the situation. Economists generally favor *exit*; they expect that the firm either will respond by eliminating slack or will be replaced by a more efficient competitor. Political scientists traditionally favor *voice*, which they believe will stimulate a positive response from those in control of the organization or will result in new leaders being chosen.

In economic organizations, Hirschman notes, people have a strong tendency to rely almost entirely on exit to deal with problems of slack performance. A person's decision to use exit or voice depends heavily on his estimate of the prospects for success and,

> while exit involves nothing but a clearcut either-or decision, voice is an art constantly evolving in new directions. This situation makes for an important bias in favor of exit when both options are present; customer-members will ordinarily base their decisions on past experience with cost and effectiveness of voice even though the possible discovery of low cost and greater effectiveness is of the very essence of voice. The presence of the exit alternative can therefore tend to atrophy the art of voice.

Hirschman's work clearly is relevant to the corporate governance situation. The preponderant reaction to declines in management quality has been exit—the disgruntled shareholder sells his stock. Exit provides a relatively low-cost and certain option, while voice— use of the proxy machinery—is apt to be expensive and of questionable effectiveness. Moreover, management tends to promote exit in order to avoid development of democratic voice mechanisms that could threaten the managers' hold on their positions. For example,

in 1978 The Business Roundtable, discussing the role of shareholders in corporate governance, stated:

> Proposals to enlarge materially shareowner participation in corporate
> governance all run into these stubborn practical difficulties, and are
> likely to be of interest only to very small and unrepresentative groups
> of corporate critics. Moreover, the ability to dispose of shares readily
> provides a practical answer in most cases to general investor concerns.

There is no need to develop new mechanisms to promote shareholders' use of voice, this group of business leaders is saying. If a
shareholder does not like what one management is doing, let him
sell his stock and buy into another corporation.

THE STOCK MARKET

Ease of exit has largely prevented development of pressure from
shareholders for reform of the corporate electoral process. It also
has held down concern by shareholders with the legitimacy of corporate management. However, unless exit serves as an adequate substitute for voice in promoting corporate efficiency, ease of exit does
not address the broader aspects of the problem of corporate legitimacy.

The argument frequently is made that shareholders do stimulate
efficient use of corporate power by "voting" in the marketplace.
When shareholders exit because of dissatisfaction with management,
the price of the company's stock declines. As a consequence, firms
with many dissatisfied shareholders will find it difficult to raise
capital, while well-managed firms will not. In addition, because a
corporation's executives often have a substantial personal financial
interest in its stock, they will sense negative market reactions to
corporate performance. Finally, supporters of governance through
exit contend, if the price of a corporation's stock drops too low in
relation to its "inherent value"—the value of the enterprise if properly managed—a tender offer by persons interested in displacing
management becomes a distinct possibility.

These arguments about the impact of the stock market on management performance all have some validity. However, they all also
suffer from defects which, taken together, dilute considerably the
legitimacy conveyed by operation of the stock market.

First of all, as noted previously, most large corporations operate
in markets that are far from perfectly competitive. Thus, poor man-

agement decisions often are not reflected accurately in immediate market results for a company's product and become evident only after extended periods of time.

Second, and most important, serious questions exist about how efficient the stock market is in pricing corporate securities. Stock prices primarily reflect expectations about how a corporation will perform. Many studies demonstrate that the market uses efficiently the information available to it, but that the information is largely historic and is not complete. Thus, it seems likely that the market will often value a corporation's securities incorrectly. As an example, consider tender offer situations, where offerers generally seem to believe that the market has undervalued a company substantially and try to exploit the market's misjudgment. Apparently tendering companies feel they can benefit from takeovers even though they must pay a substantial premium over the value the stock market has placed on target corporations. This premium, most observers believe, cannot be explained as reflecting the difference between a target company's inherent value and its market value because frequently the best run companies, rather than those with inept and inefficient managements, are the most sought after takeover targets.

Third, the impact of market forces often is diluted or delayed, thus reducing management's sensitivity to exit. If a firm can generate internally the funds needed to finance its capital projects, low stock prices exert only a weak influence on its management, even if the return on reinvested earnings is well below that available from other investments. Similarly, in the product marketplace, the ultimate deterrent of bankruptcy comes into play only with respect to the most inefficient or inept. It usually occurs only after an extended period of decline.

Fourth, the incentive compensation plans for executives in many corporations ensure substantial payouts even in the absence of any appreciation in the price of the corporation's stock. Studies show little relationship between profitability and pay levels. Thus, the nexus between stock prices and management's personal interests is often weak.

Finally, to the extent that many corporations suffer from similar weaknesses, be they inefficient management or management overreaching, the impact of exit may be blunted, despite any potential management sensitivity to it. Dissatisfied shareholders may move in relatively uniform numbers from one unsatisfactory firm to another, aware of the problems they have left behind but hoping naively that "the grass is greener" where they are going. So long as entrances and exits remain roughly in balance, exit will have little impact.

THE LEGAL SYSTEM

Demonstrated weaknesses in the corporate electoral process and in the impact of the stock market on corporate governance give heightened importance to the potential contribution of corporate law to the governance system. Corporate law, supported by the SEC's disclosure requirements, has demonstrated some effectiveness. Still, it is the limits of the legal mechanism, not its strengths, that must be stressed.

The flaw here is not, as it was with the electoral process, that the system makes assertion of legal rights by shareholders economically unattractive. True, the costs of litigation often are substantial, and a shareholder-plaintiff, if he is successful in a derivative suit, benefits from the litigation only in proportion to his stock interest in the corporation. However, there is another element in the litigation process that destroys the parallel with the electoral process—awards of attorneys' fees. In order to furnish an incentive for shareholders to assert their legal rights, corporate law provides that corporations pay attorneys' fees for shareholders who are successful in derivative suits. The chemistry—or alchemy—of the shareholder-counsel relationship is a subject that need not detain us here. Suffice it to say that the prospect of awards of attorneys' fees has helped encourage shareholder derivative suits.

However, while corporate law provides an incentive to sue, it does not make suits easy to win. Rather, there has been a "race for the bottom" in which state governments, interested in increasing their revenues from corporate franchise taxes and recognizing that decisions on where to incorporate usually are made by corporate managements, have developed laws that minimize the responsibilities and liabilities of managers to their shareholders and also reduce shareholders' power over management. The acknowledged winner in this competition has been Delaware. The legislature and courts of that state, sensitive to the financial and other benefits the state obtains as the domicile of so many corporations, have developed a body of legal doctrines that has steadily eroded the obligations of managers. Because legislatures and courts in other states are unwilling to cede the field entirely to Delaware and know that the U.S. Constitution requires every state to treat foreign and domestic corporations equally and to give "full faith and credit" to the laws of the state in which an enterprise is incorporated, they have felt compelled to follow Delaware's lead.

Duty of Due Care—Directors' duty of due care has been interpreted almost out of existence. While state statutes provide that directors' decisions be judged by the standard of what reasonably prudent men would have done in similar circumstances, courts have interpreted this standard as requiring directors to devote only very modest amounts of time and effort to managing or overseeing a company's business. The courts also have held that where a director has been negligent, he will be held liable only when a shareholder can prove that the corporation suffered losses due to the director's negligence and that the losses were not due to other factors—a burden of proof that it often is impossible for a shareholder to meet. When losses are due not to negligence but to miscalculation, directors are protected by the business judgment rule, which holds that they will be liable only for misjudgments that involve elements of fraud or illegality. As described by one expert commentator, Joseph Bishop, Jr. writing in the *Yale Law Journal* in 1968, the result is that "cases in which directors of industrial corporations have been held liable for negligence uncomplicated by self-dealing [represent] . . . a very small number of needles in a very large haystack."

An illustration of how ridiculous the situation has become is provided by *Kamin v. American Express* (1976). American Express wanted to dispose of a large block of stock of Donaldson, Lufkin & Jenrette, Inc. (DLJ) in which it had a paper loss of about $26 million. If American Express sold the stock, it would be able to offset the loss against capital gains and save about $8 million in taxes. However, the loss on the sale would have to be accounted for by reducing the net income figure in American Express' financial statement for the years of the sale. Alternatively, American Express could distribute the DLJ stock as a dividend to its shareholders. The loss then could be accounted for by a charge against accumulated surplus, but there would be no tax saving.

The directors of American Express decided to distribute the DLJ stock as a dividend rather than to sell it. Allegedly they did so because they believed that distribution would have a less adverse impact on the price of American Express stock, even though the economic substance of the transaction would be disclosed fully and it would be clear that the corporation had foregone a potential $8 million tax saving.

Without even a cursory analysis of the seemingly ridiculous assumptions on which the directors had based their decision, the court dismissed the shareholder's complaint. The directors' decision, the court stated, was insulated from judicial scrutiny by the business judgment rule.

Duty of Loyalty—Courts have given somewhat more weight to legal prohibitions against self-dealing by directors, but still the system provides directors with power that has often been used to the detriment of a corporation or its minority shareholders. The unsatisfactory aspects of the legal rules in this area have been detailed by many commentators, including William Cary in a landmark study published in the *Yale Law Journal* in 1974. Rather than ensuring that a director's single, or even principal, objective will be to advance the interests of shareholders, the law allows directors considerable discretion in deciding how to divide up the surplus generated by a corporation's activities. Often they allocate a very generous portion of that surplus to top management, thereby limiting the funds available to advance shareholders' interests. In fact, Cary suggests, the situation has deteriorated to the point where large numbers of people may be loathe to entrust their savings to the tender mercies of corporate managers. The ability of companies to raise capital may be threatened as a result.

A CENTRAL FLAW

Serious as the defects in the principal mechanisms of the corporate governance system are, they tend to mask a more basic flaw—the fact that the system is oriented almost entirely toward promoting competitive efficiency. Public concern about aspects of corporate activity not accounted for by the market has increased, and governmental measures adopted to regulate corporate social behavior have not significantly limited managerial discretion. The present governance system, however, largely ignores both nonmarket aspects of corporate behavior and the public policies embodied in regulatory programs. It deals only with an artificial legal entity—the "corporation"—and attempts to establish an appropriate relationship among the constituents of that entity—shareholders, directors, and corporate officers. Only shareholders, and neither the state nor any of the other groups affected by corporate activity, are allowed to vote in corporate elections. Yet shareholders are not expected to represent the public's interest in any value other than competitive efficiency.

Similarly, the stock market is not concerned with social values except insofar as they are translated into economic costs. In situations where the stock market operates somewhat efficiently, it may even increase the social costs generated by a firm's activities. For example, if, as some observers argue, the decline in the fortunes of the American steel industry is due largely to inept management, the market can be said to be operating efficiently by denying new capital to steel companies and depressing the price of their shares. But the market takes no account of and may even exacerbate the adverse effects that inefficient performance is having on a variety of constituencies, including the employees of those companies, the communities in which they are located, the national economy, and the country's foreign relations.

Corporate law also tends to disregard the interests of the non-shareholder constituents of corporations. Only shareholders of a corporation can sue directors for not performing properly, and they are limited to vindicating economic interests. For example, during the Vietnam War, when a shareholder of Honeywell, Inc. attempted to examine certain of the company's books and records for the purpose of promoting the election of directors who would oppose Honeywell's continued production of antipersonnel weapons, the Supreme Court of Minnesota denied his claim on the grounds that his interests in the company were strictly social, and that the courts will recognize as valid only shareholders' economic interests (Pillsbury v. Honeywell, Inc. [1974]).

The U. S. Supreme Court had an opportunity to reach a very different result in *Cort v. Ash* (1975), a class action brought by a shareholder of Bethlehem Steel claiming that corporate funds had been used illegally to pay for a partisan political advertisement. If the Court had held that a shareholder suit could be based solely on a finding that the federal election laws had been violated, it might have opened the door to shareholder suits brought to ensure corporate compliance with a variety of other public policies. But the Court decided, by a 9-0 vote, that the shareholder's suit had to be based on some claimed violation of directors' fiduciary duties. Thus it made litigation of this kind subject to the problems that plague all suits claiming directors have violated their duty of due care, including the problem of showing that directors' disregard of a public policy caused a financial loss to the corporation.

LIMITS TO LEGITIMACY

The corporate governance system is deeply flawed. The mechanisms that are supposed to channel use of corporate power all operate imperfectly, despite the assistance they receive from disclosure requirements. The electoral process usually is little more than a sham and certainly does not operate to assure accountability. The stock market exerts a significant influence, but it also suffers from many serious defects. The legal system plays close to a meaningless role in compelling directors to use their power wisely, but is somewhat more effective in deterring self- dealing by directors. As a whole the system primarily seeks to assure competitive-efficiency and in so doing ignores the interests that many nonshareholder groups have in how directors use their power. Members of these groups are demanding a voice within corporations because they cannot readily exit from their relationships with them. They are particularly perturbed by the ways in which self-selected corporate managers appear free to make decisions that affect their lives.

In sum, the corporate governance system fails to fulfill its central purpose—providing legitimacy to those who hold positions of power within corporations. It does not effectively make them accountable to either shareholders or society. As the system's failure becomes more widely recognized, pressures for dramatic changes in the governance system are likely to increase. Those who control corporations may find their legitimacy first challenged and then lost. As Kenneth Boulding has observed, "disillusionment is a very powerful source of delegitimation; and trying to build legitimacy on detectable illusions is a very dangerous game, which has affected both government and business."

A Role for Disclosure

We come, then, to the question of how disclosure might be used to deal with the problems in the corporate governance system. Of course, "disclosure" is not a particularly precise concept. In considering the effectiveness and potential of disclosure, we shall limit ourselves to discussion of requirements that publicly-held corporations make available information concerning their activities to their shareholders and, consequently, to the public. Issuing disclosure requirements of this kind has been one of the principal responsibilities of the SEC.

HOW DISCLOSURE HAS WORKED

The SEC-administered disclosure system has performed two functions. First, it has greatly facilitated the operation of the principal mechanisms of the corporate governance system. While a few commentators have suggested that, absent an SEC, market forces would have brought forth the kinds of information now made public pursuant to the SEC's disclosure requirements, most share the view that whatever the defects are in the corporation governance system, they would be much worse in the absence of SEC-mandated disclosures. Corporate elections, if anything, would be even less meaningful; the stock market would price securities less accurately; the legal system would be less successful in ensuring care and preventing self-dealing.

Second, where disclosure supports accountability, the existence of disclosure requirements has deterred a good deal of undesirable corporate conduct. For example, by requiring disclosure about a corporation's business dealings with its directors, the SEC has caused directors of corporations to abandon many transactions of questionable propriety. It is here, primarily, that the sunlight shed as a result of disclosure requirements has been a potent disinfectant.

On the other hand, disclosure has not been a cure-all. Information alone has not made ineffective governance mechanisms effective. Perhaps most importantly, the requirement that financial results be reported accurately has not vitalized the electoral process or enforcement of directors' duty of due care. Neither, frequently, has it kept managers from continuing inept performance.

Also, the SEC has usually declined to use disclosure to address the interests of nonshareholder constituencies. The Commission conceives its responsibility as meeting the information needs of investors and shareholders and has concluded, after extensive hearings on the subject, that those needs relate primarily to matters of economic significance.

In one instance, the SEC initiated a program to require disclosure of information that was not clearly significant in an economic sense —data about corporations' "questionable payments" to foreign agents and officials of foreign governments. The program became embroiled in controversy. The SEC and supporters of the program argued that the data to be disclosed cast important light on the quality of a company's management, the integrity of its accounting procedures, and the nature of its business relationships. Critics contended that most of the information the SEC required be disclosed was of no economic significance and that the SEC was improperly using disclosure primarily to influence corporate behavior. The SEC denied the first charge but acknowledged that it wanted to discourage companies from making questionable payments.

No complete evaluation has been made of the impact of this SEC disclosure program. The evidence suggests, though, that the disclosures required by the SEC did not have much influence on corporate elections. No incumbent directors or officers of corporations that admitted making questionable payments were deposed as a consequence of campaigns launched by dissident shareholders, and few of the numerous shareholder proposals that challenged unusual payments received great support.

Further, one study has found little shift in stock prices as a result of disclosures of questionable payments. Shareholder challenges by litigation to these payments (as opposed to clearly illegal political contributions) have met with little success.

However, it is also clear that the requirement for disclosure of questionable payments has had a substantial impact on corporate activities, perhaps because the actions disclosed—payments of what often appeared to be bribes or kickbacks—were intended to distort the operation of the mechanism on which corporations base their principal claim to legitimacy—the market for the goods and services they produce. Thus Roderick M. Hills, while chairman of the SEC, in 1976 hearings on corporate rights and responsibilities, spoke out against

> management [that] is too often complacent, self-perpetuating and un-
> responsible. When reported profits decline to such an extent as to
> threaten the serenity of their well paid isolation, some managers are
> tempted to change their accounting, the figures or the morals of their
> company in order to present a more pleasing profit picture. . . .

Responding to this and similar sentiments, in some of the most extreme situations corporate boards removed the executives who had been responsible for unusual or illegal payments. In many more companies, policies and procedures were revised to prevent future questionable payments of a kind that would be subject to the SEC's disclosure requirements.

DISCLOSURE AND THE GOVERNANCE SYSTEM

Turning to the question of whether changes should be made in the disclosure system, it seems most sensible to consider first, disclosure's potential to improve the governance system with shareholders, and then to review how disclosure might be used to respond to the interests of nonshareholder constituencies. We shall look first at how disclosure might improve the operation of the stock market.

Disclosure and the Stock Market—The stock market has been shown to use information efficiently. To price securities more accurately, it needs additional information.

The SEC has developed extensive disclosure requirements to meet the needs of the stock market, including requirements that companies make available such refined data as the details of compensating bank balances, of unfunded pension liabilities, and of accrued leasehold obligations. In addition, the Commission has interpreted its antifraud rules to hold corporate insiders responsible for ensuring that all material information is made available to the stock market and to prevent them from earning extraordinary profits in the market by holding information back from the public.

The Commission's approach to disclosure of financial information was reviewed in 1976–77 by its Advisory Committee on Corporate Disclosure. The Committee concluded that the needs of the market could be served better if three major changes were made in the disclosure system. First, since so many corporations engage in multiple lines of business, the SEC should require corporations to provide more detailed reports about their activities in each of their principal lines of business. Second, the SEC should urge corporations to present more detailed analysis and evaluation of their financial results. This recommendation reflected the Committee's view that management usually is far more able than outsiders to interpret the information that the corporation makes available to the market. Finally, because expectations about the future are the basis of most investment decisions, the Committee suggested that the SEC encourage companies to publish projections of future financial performance in addition to the historic data that had been the focus of the SEC's reporting requirements. In early 1978 the SEC announced that it intended to act positively on all three recommendations.

The proposed revisions in the disclosure system should improve the market's ability to price stocks accurately, but they will fall far short of creating a perfect market. Many problems in the market's pricing of stock are structural and cannot be solved by increasing the availability of information and opinion. The information to be disclosed under the proposed disclosure regulations is considerably more subjective than data that the SEC required be disclosed in the past. There will be greater variations in the quality of information made available by different firms and thus, continued distortions in the market's assessment of individual corporations.

Even if highly accurate pricing of securities were achieved, the stock market would still have defects as a governance mechanism. Disclosure can make exit a more powerful decision, but steps also are needed to bring added vitality to the two mechanisms that rely on voice—the electoral process and the requirements of corporate law.

Disclosure and the Electoral Process—The principal weaknesses of the electoral process are structural, stemming from the ease and certainty of exit and the high cost and questionable efficacy of voice. All these encourage shareholder passivity.

No changes in the corporate electoral mechanism are likely to change this situation dramatically, just as changes in the laws relating to political campaigns are not likely to convert passive citizens into active political campaigners. Moreover, even with greater "corporate democracy," shareholders can never substitute effectively for managers of large corporations.

These observations do not mandate against efforts to revive the electoral process. Rather, they serve to highlight the kinds of changes needed—changes directed not at stimulating massive shareholder activism and not at substituting participative decision-making for professional management, but at the one part of the electoral process where shareholders clearly have a valid role to play: election of the board of directors. The board can perform a vital function by monitoring the performance of operating management for shareholders and thus providing greater legitimacy to how management uses a corporation's resources.

To encourage more shareholder involvement in the selection of directors, the cost of participation in the electoral process must be reduced. One way to reduce costs is to require corporations to disclose more information about their boards—information that will allow at least reasonably sophisticated investors to understand how well a board of directors is functioning and to compare the operations of boards of different companies. Costs also could be reduced by providing shareholders with increased access to corporation's proxy materials, which would allow them to communicate more easily with other shareholders.

That better information and improved access will increase constructive shareholder participation in the process by which directors are elected is suggested by experience during the 1970s with shareholder proposals raising social issues. In 1972, and again in 1976, the SEC amended its proxy rules to make it easier for shareholders concerned about the social aspects of corporate performance to have their own proposals included in corporations' proxy materials. Many more shareholder proposals appeared.

Over the same period, relatively low-cost sources of information about the social issues being raised in shareholder proposals were developed. As a consequence, many institutional investors began to discuss the proposals more and to take informed positions on them. Previously these institutions had not paid much attention because they were not familiar with the issues involved and could not justify the expense of doing independent research.

With improved rights of access and greater institutional participation in the voting process, several shareholder groups gained the attention of corporate management. In several instances they persuaded management to take their views into account, even though in all cases the activities failed to get close to majority support for their proposals from fellow shareholders. Shareholder activists, business leaders, and interested professional observers all acknowledge that the shareholder proposal process, as it operated during the 1970s, was often beneficial to corporations.

Similar changes should be made in the process by which corporate directors are elected. The SEC should require corporations to include in their proxy material nominees from shareholders for election as directors. Such a change in the proxy rules is within the power of the SEC and would not conflict with state laws. It clearly would facilitate shareholder participation in the electoral process, breaking the near monopoly that managements now have on communications about selection of directors.

To limit frivolity and abuse, the SEC should limit the number of nominees that any shareholder could suggest. It might also require a modest initial demonstration of support (perhaps nomination by shareholders owning stock worth at least $100,000) before a company would be required to list a shareholder nominee in its proxy statement. It could require shareholders to reimburse some part of the costs incurred by a company in circulating a nomination if the nominee did not receive at least a minimal level of support—say 3 percent of the votes cast.

The SEC also should require corporations to disclose more information about their boards to help shareholders decide whether a corporation's directors have served or are likely to serve as independent monitors of management's performance. We shall not detail here our suggestions for disclosure requirements that will accomplish this purpose, for they have been published elsewhere. (Elliott J. Weiss and Donald E. Schwartz, "Disclosure Approach for Directors," *Harvard Business Review* [1978].) Suffice it to say that disclosure about boards should include information about

1. individual nominees for election to a board, including their affiliation with management, compensation received, time spent at board and committee meetings, and other directorships;
2. procedures and criteria used to select nominees, including the extent to which a board controls management's solicitation of proxies;
3. the organization and activities of a board, including the membership and authority of board committees, the flow of information to the board, the procedures and criteria used by the board to monitor management's performance, and staff assistance provided to the board; and
4. the reasons why directors have resigned from a board or declined to stand for reelection.

The changes we have suggested, if implemented by the SEC, stand a good chance of stimulating significant participation in the selection of directors by the most sophisticated and quality-conscious shareholders, the members of an organization, Hirschman notes, who are likely to be most effective in using voice but who also are likely to be the first to exit when problems develop. As experience with shareholder proposals demonstrates, the participation of this select group—even when the mass of shareholders remains inactive—can influence and benefit corporations.

Requiring disclosure about boards of directors, by itself, is likely to have constructive effects. Disclosure about their duties and performance will motivate corporate directors, already sensitive to their legal responsibilities and perhaps even more to their public images, to behave more responsibly and more independently. Corporate managers, unwilling to acknowledge that they often have dominated the directors to whom they are supposed to be accountable, will be pressed to relax their hold.

Disclosure and Corporate Law—Changes in the election process are likely to affect the manner in which directors meet their obligations of loyalty and due care, but they will not affect the legal standards by which directors' conduct is evaluated. Without additional changes in state law or in related disclosure requirements, those standards remain inadequate.

As discussed previously, substantial incentives exist to encourage reliance on the legal mechanisms of corporate governance which constitute a sort of voice. The problem is that too much of what directors do is insulated from the reach of voice. No serious critics of the system maintain that responsibility for running a corporate business should be transferred to some other entity such as a court. The critics' argument is that the conduct of directors and managers should be judged by more stringent standards.

Most criticisms can only be met by substantive changes in corporate law. Limited improvement can be made by using the SEC's disclosure authority imaginatively.

Specifically, the SEC can ensure that the disadvantages of all transactions that customarily are submitted to shareholders for their approval and that involve some element of conflict of interest between the corporation and its management are fully and conspicuously discussed in proxy statements. While customarily acquiescent shareholders still may often say "yes" to such proposals, better disclosure may lead them to say "no." Management may think about disclosure and not propose at all. Even where transactions are approved, the information elicited by the disclosure requirements may provide grist for the litigation mill.

The SEC is aware that disclosure might be used this way. For example, in so-called "going private" transactions, where the dominant shareholders of a corporation use their position to squeeze out all other shareholders, the SEC has proposed that the corporation be required to include in its proxy statement extremely detailed information of a kind that is likely to be very helpful to a shareholder who wants to attack the fairness of the transaction, such as information about alternatives considered by management and data demonstrating how management arrived at the price to be offered to minority shareholders.

If one shares the SEC's conviction that state law does not adequately protect the interests of minority shareholders in going private transactions, it seems clear that the proposed disclosures, if made, would greatly increase controlling shareholders' vulnerability to successful derivative suits. And, of course, if the required information is not fully and accurately disclosed, minority shareholders could bring suit under the antifraud provisions of the federal securities law.

The going private situation, however, also highlights the danger of relying largely on disclosure to remedy weaknesses in state corporate laws. The locus of policy-making about the propriety of certain kinds of transactions is shifted, in fact if not in law, from legislative and judicial bodies to the SEC. Many commentators, for example, feel the SEC is misguided in its hostility to going private transactions and believe that the proposed disclosure requirements will burden unduly many legitimate transactions. Yet, given a situation in which many believe state corporate law in general to be inadequate, it is difficult to restrain the SEC from using its disclosure authority to sabotage transactions that, although legal under state law, the Commission considers to be particularly objectionable.

What transactions are, or should be, on the SEC's "hit list" could fuel a lively debate. Among the contenders, depending on one's point of view, would be management perquisites, certain incentive compensation plans, and measures to frustrate tender offers (colorfully known to the corporate bar as "shark repellants"). On these and other transactions, though, to prevent self-dealing by management, disclosure can only partially compensate for weaknesses in the corporate laws of different states.

DISCLOSURE AND OTHER CONSTITUENCIES

Improvements in the electoral and legal mechanisms of corporate governance, by changes in the SEC proxy and disclosure rules or by amendments to laws that establish fiduciary obligations for directors, can enhance the legitimacy of corporate management vis-à-vis shareholders, but they would not respond in any meaningful way to the concerns of external constituencies. They all are oriented toward the conventional view of corporations, which enfranchises no one but shareholders and allows no opportunity for nonshareholder groups to exercise voice within corporations.

To promote corporate responsiveness to the interests of nonshareholder groups, giving these groups a voice within corporations seems more attractive than approaching the problem with traditional forms of government regulation. Indeed, the arguments in favor of changing the corporate governance system to provide nonshareholder interests with a voice within corporations appear to be compelling. However, even sympathetic observers find practical and conceptual difficulties with the specific alternatives to the existing governance system that have been proposed, such as allowing designated nonshareholder groups to elect directors or providing for a few public directors in large or troublesome corporations. Consequently, people have begun to consider disclosure as a mechanism for responding to the interests of nonshareholder constituencies.

On reflection, though, it can be seen that disclosure requirements unrelated to the existing mechanisms of corporate governance—the corporate electoral process, corporate law, and the operation of the capital market—are not likely to have much impact on corporate conduct. Disclosure has worked well only where it has been linked to a meaningful governance mechanism. Wherever disclosure was not likely to lead to some definable legal or economic consequence, it has been effective only where it generated social pressures to which those in control of corporations were sensitive, as has been the case with questionable payments and is likely to be true with regard to boards of directors. However, in most areas of social concern about corporate activity, corporate executives and their peers are not in sympathy with the goals of nonshareholder groups or of the regulatory programs they have supported.

For example, in its 1978 discussion of *The Role and Composition of the Board of Directors of the Large Publicly Owned Corporation,* The Business Roundtable made clear its view that "other groups affected by corporate activities cannot be placed on a plane with owners" when corporate decisions are made that involve conflicts between those groups' interests and the interests of shareholders. Similarly, the Roundtable highlighted its concern about "excessive and unnecessary costs" imposed on corporations by legal requirements and regulatory programs. Clearly, disclosure requirements about social performance, unrelated to potential legal consequences, are unlikely to have much impact on business leaders who share the Roundtable's views.

In addition, the tough practical problems that have bedeviled every proposal to expand the constituencies represented within the corporation apply with at least equal force to designing most requirements for disclosure of corporate social performance, particularly if similar requirements are to be applicable to all publicly-held corporations. In what areas is disclosure to be required? When the SEC asked this in 1974, groups suggested mandated disclosure about more than 100 new areas of corporate activity. Winnowing such a list down to manageable size presents a formidable task, particularly in the absence of objective standards or legislated priorities, and it also would place too much discretionary power in the hands of the SEC.

In each area of social concern, what specific information should corporations be required to disclose about their performance? In a few areas, such as equal employment opportunity, a simple statistical presentation is feasible and may have a constructive impact, but even there serious questions can be raised about the significance of the data. In most areas of social concern, developing meaningful objective measures becomes very complex. What data, for example, would provide an accurate picture of efforts in a multiproduct corporation to prevent occupational health problems from developing among its employees? Should the information include employee health statistics, research findings, expenditures for health research, medical screening of employees, amount of corporate investment in protective equipment or in reduction of hazards, findings of government agencies and company responses thereto, or lists of health hazards to which employees are or may be exposed and descriptions of a company's strategy for dealing with those hazards? How could the system assure that the disclosure requirements would allow meaningful comparisons of performance across firms?

Finally, how would disclosure reveal the truly important facts about adaptation of managerial structures and behavior? Robert Ackerman, in *The Social Challenge to Business,* has shown that corporations typically respond to a social demand by going through an extended three-stage process of adapting their management structure to meet that demand. In light of Ackerman's findings, the most significant measure of corporate responsiveness in any area of social concern would be a description of how far along the company was in the adaptation process. Designing disclosure rules which would regularly and reliably describe management processes presents an impossible task.

In sum, new mandatory disclosure requirements do not appear able to address effectively the demands of the nonshareholder constituencies of corporations. If the corporate governance system is to take more account of the interests of these groups, changes should be made first in the substantive aspects of the system. Until such changes are made, it would be unwise and probably unfeasible for the SEC or any comparable agency to develop, as an adjunct to the corporate governance system, mandatory requirements that corporations disclose information about matters that are significant primarily for social, as opposed to economic, reasons. To the extent that information about corporate social performance is needed to assist in the implementation of regulatory programs or to arouse the public about social problems caused by corporate activities, the task of developing that information should be left to specialized regulatory agencies or to the mass media.

Corporations who wish to demonstrate their responsiveness to social concerns can volunteer information. In fact, in most instances corporate managers are well situated to understand the social problems their companies' activities are creating and to explain effectively how they are addressing those problems. A continuing commitment by corporations to report fully and frankly about these matters, carried through without deceit or artifice and backed up by action to address the problems, might go a long way toward alleviating public concerns about the legitimacy of corporate managers. Here, though, sunlight's potential as a disinfectant appears to rest on the possibility of voluntary exposure.

Laurence I. Moss

4

Corporate Governance
and the
Environmental Movement

My work of the past few years, especially that connected with the National Coal Policy Project, has given me a perspective on certain aspects of corporate governance in relation to the environmental movement.

The environmental movement raises a number of issues that affect corporate governance. It seeks to avoid or reduce adverse environmental impacts—pollution of air and water, disturbance of unique ecosystems, infringement on scenic and natural areas—that corporations can and do produce. The environmental movement also seeks to avoid uneconomic use of natural resources. "Uneconomic use" refers to a situation where the cost of using the resource is greater than the value added by its use.

The appeals of environmentalists, and the resistance of many corporations to them, have produced much acrimony. Either because of, or in spite of this confrontation, our nation has made a number of important legislative and administrative decisions that have begun and will continue to yield progress toward the goals of

LAURENCE I. MOSS *is a consultant on energy and environmental policy. He is chairman of the Environmental Caucus of the National Coal Policy Project and has served as president of the Sierra Club and chairman of the Federal Energy Administration's Environmental Advisory Committee.*

environmentalists. But a nagging question persists: might progress have been faster and less costly if a cooperative exploration of alternative policies had been conducted?

The National Coal Policy Project

About two years ago, it occurred to a few members of the environmental and industrial communities that the two groups had, so to speak, "business to transact" and that the only available forums for conducting that business were adversarial in nature. They asked if it might be possible to create a nonadversarial forum in which policies acceptable to both sides could be fashioned and recommended to decision-makers.

The National Coal Policy Project (NCPP) grew out of that interest. It has involved more than sixty participants, half named by each side. Five task forces were created to cover the spectrum of coal-related environmental and energy policy issues. They were: Mining, Transportation (of coal), Air Pollution, Full Utilization and Conservation, and Energy Pricing. An ad hoc task force on emissions charges was later formed from the membership of the Air Pollution and Pricing task forces.

Each of the five task forces met six to eight times during the course of 1977. The governing board of the project was the Plenary Group, made up of the co-chairman and co-vice chairman of each of the task forces; two consultants, one named by each side; a neutral chairman (Francis X. Quinn of Temple University); and the two caucus chairmen, Gerald Decker (Corporate Energy Manager of Dow Chemical) and myself. The Plenary Group met on five occasions.

The written product of the first phase of the project consists of a 900-page report containing more than 200 policy recommendations. The participants were not able to resolve all of their initial disagreements. No one expected them to do so. But they were pleasantly surprised that they could resolve as many as they did.

The purpose of this chapter is to explore certain questions of corporate governance, not to delve into the recommendations of the NCPP. It may, nevertheless, be useful to give an idea of the scope of the recommendations by citing a few highlights. The group agreed that:

1. Coal can be mined in some areas of the U.S. without too much

damage to the environment if proper procedures are used. In other areas the problems are greater, and only carefully controlled and limited experimental mining should be allowed until solutions are found.

2. The proper pricing of energy, including its associated environmental and social costs, is urgent. Low prices for energy lead to waste and pollution. Proper pricing, based on the cost of the most expensive units needed to meet demand, would generate powerful market forces to work toward a more efficient allocation of resources. It would reduce both adverse impacts and the need for detailed government regulation.

3. Major coal-burning facilities (power plants, gasification facilities, etc.) should be located in the general areas of the ultimate users of the energy and not in remote regions.

4. The Environmental Protection Agency (EPA) should be allowed to authorize variances for some first-of-a-kind coal-burning plants specifically to encourage development and use of innovative combustion and pollution abatement technology. In such cases, a failure to limit emissions to those standards normally allowed would not be grounds for shutting down the plant. Instead, up to a level specified by the EPA, continued operation would be permitted with payment of charges proportional to the excess emissions.

5. A consolidated hearing process would facilitate state decisions on specific sites. This process should include early notification of plans and alternatives, and public funding for responsible citizen groups to hire experts and participate more effectively.

6. An emission charge and rebate plan, the major elements of which we have outlined, should be tried in an area of the country where air quality standards are not now being met.

7. User charges to cover the full costs of waterways and highways should be assessed on commercial users. The waterway charges should be constituted so that each segment of the waterway system supports its own costs.

8. Economic regulation by government of the transportation sector should be sharply curtailed. Railroads should be permitted to enter into long-term contracts for the hauling of coal, and coal slurry pipelines should be given powers of eminent domain if needed to cross railroad rights of way.

9. The government should not subsidize—through grants, loan guarantees, etc.—the so called "commercialization" of large cen-

tralized energy supply facilities, since such subsidies disguise the true cost of energy and lead to its uneconomic use.

10. Mandatory coal conversion orders should be paced to encourage the use of cleaner and more efficient coal-using technology, for example, that using low-Btu gasification and the cogeneration of electricity along with heat and steam where that is a feasible option.

The report, of course, contains much more detail on these and other recommendations.

Whether or not the recommendations gain wide acceptance, it is undeniable that the work of the NCPP stands in sharp contrast to the polarization and acrimony that has characterized the national debate over energy and environmental policy.

Separation of Policy-Making from Technical Functions

In selecting participants for the NCPP, attempts were made to choose individuals who combined technical expertise with policy-making responsibilities. It proved easier to identify such people in environmental than in industrial organizations. This is, perhaps, a function of the relative lack of resources of environmental organizations; the key people on each issue are required to cover many bases. The hierarchical arrangement and separation of functions typical of the large corporation make it uncertain whether the technical experts can influence corporate policy.

This dilemma was not entirely resolved. The industrial side did choose some individuals with primarily policy-making responsibilities and some with technical responsibilities, in the belief that the collective body could perform both functions well. I believe, in fact, that it did. But the acid test is yet to come: will the agreed-upon recommendations of the NCPP have a significant effect on corporate policy? The answer will depend, in part, on the effectiveness of the mechanisms for communication within the corporation. Thus far, only a few chief executives have publicly endorsed the processes and recommendations of the project. Unless more support from the corporate world is obtained, the NCPP may go down in history as an interesting experiment that failed. With such support it can become a path-finding exploration of new processes pointing the way to policies more acceptable to *both* sides than those produced through exclusive reliance on confrontation.

The Problem of the Washington Representative

The difficulty of obtaining widespread support, in the environmental as well as the industrial communities, is compounded by an institutional problem. The interests of Washington representatives do not always coincide with the interests of the organizations that are represented.

For example, a particular organization, not one of the national environmental organizations with a large grass-roots membership, acts as the Washington representative of the national organizations on certain issues. One of these issues was legislation controlling strip mining of coal. Their key people were invited to play leading roles in the NCPP. They declined. In fact, they attempted (with only limited success) to dissuade their colleagues in other organizations from participating.

They were sent copies of the draft reports of the NCPP's Mining Task Force. Environmental members of the task force asked these people to let them know if they objected to any of the emerging recommendations or if there were recommendations not made that should be included. They declined to respond.

Finally, shortly before the NCPP recommendations were to be released to the public, the Washington group prepared a critique of the Mining Task Force recommendations, accusing the task force of undermining the new strip mine law. The critique was presented to the Sierra Club's Board of Directors to convince them that they should disavow the NCPP recommendations. (The board, incidentally, took no such action.) We obtained a copy of the critique (by asking for it at the public meeting) and, though it was very late in terms of the processes of the NCPP, reworded certain of our recommendations to reduce the possibility of the misinterpretation and misrepresentation that we believed had occurred. The industrial members cooperated in this effort.

The revisions had no effect on the criticism; after public release, members of the organization in question continued to cite and oppose the wording of the old (and unreleased) draft. It became obvious that *the criticisms had nothing to do with our recommendations!* What was really bothering this organization was the prospect of a diminished role for the Washington representative.

The Washington representative, as a conduit of information and the person closest to the scene, is in a unique position to influence the policies of the organizations that are represented. The basis of the NCPP, on the other hand, was that direct communication among the principals of the opposing groups would lead to better understanding and a measure of agreement. Even should the Washington representative be a participant, it is logical for him or her to assume that the process will not be as controllable as was the previous state of affairs. There will be, in effect, a sharing of power, and for those who care a lot about power (i.e., most of those on the Washington scene), a diminishment of the psychic satisfactions of the job.

Although my example is taken from the environmental side, I caution you that the problem extends elsewhere. I note that the leadership of the national organization of CEO's has expressed an interest in using the good offices of the organization to inform other CEO's about the project and enlist their support. Thus far, the Washington staff has been singularly unproductive on this matter.

Energy and environmental policy issues are too important for the generalists to leave the field entirely to the professional lobbyists.

Dispelling Stereotypes

One of the benefits of the NCPP, quite apart from the specifics of the recommendations, was that many stereotypes were dispelled. For example, those environmentalists who regarded industry as monolithic and intransigent on matters of environmental protection were disabused of that notion. They welcomed the diversity of interests and values present on the industrial side.

Some of the industrialists had believed that environmentalists opposed economic growth and the introduction of new technology, and favored detailed governmental regulation over marketplace solutions. They found that the environmental participants in the NCPP were not opposed to economic growth in itself, but to a pattern of growth that produced uneconomic use of natural resources and unacceptable environmental and social impact. The environmental participants favored new technology that improved efficiency and reduced resource consumption and adverse social and environmental impact. They preferred to rely on the marketplace to allocate resources where markets were workably competitive and significant external environmental and social costs were not a factor. When such were important, the environmentalists were eager to search for ways of influencing the market, short of detailed regulation, that would achieve the desired goals.

Most people in the industrial community seem to be unaware of the tradition out of which most environmentalists come. In my own case, the first serious involvement in the environmental movement was in opposing the plans of the Federal Bureau of Reclamation to build dams in the Grand Canyon. Later, I was a cofounder of the Coalition Against the SST, which led the successful campaign against the Department of Transportation's subsidy of the American SST. Still later, I initiated the lawsuit which established that the EPA (which claimed otherwise) had a duty to prevent significant deterioration of air quality. Similar experiences lead environmentalists to question whether turning more decision making over to government will necessarily solve environmental problems. It is often more difficult to move a government agency than a private company away from a preconceived position. The assumption is that the agency (by definition) is acting in the public interest; so they are given a certain benefit of the doubt not granted the private company. Moreover, on certain matters the agency acts as both judge and jury, thereby complicating the task of obtaining effective review.

How to Influence the Marketplace

Most environmentalists in this country, having similar experiences, are sympathetic to a vigorous and productive private sector. Yet the question remains as to how to influence the marketplace when it is not competitive (as with the transmission and distribution of electricity) or when it does not, by itself, value "public goods."

Public goods are those that are accessible to all and for which no private property rights can be or have been created. Public highways and waterways, and clean air and water are examples. When little or no charge is made for the use of such goods, as is now the case, users will naturally favor the use of public goods over private goods for which they must pay. It is in the economic interest of shippers to use "free" waterways and "low cost" highways instead of railroads. Similarly, it is in the economic interest of polluters to use the "free" air as a dumping ground instead of paying for scrubbers. Their use of the public goods imposes costs on others, as with higher taxes needed for the construction and maintenance of waterways and roads, and the health and other costs incurred by those exposed to pollutants.

Progress has been made, especially in the last few years, in identifying certain social costs and prescribing minimum standards of conduct, i.e., regulations, in the use of public goods. The cost of meeting the regulations then becomes the price of using the public good. This is appropriate and necessary, but not sufficient. We should make more use of economic incentives and disincentives to harness private profit in the public interest.

This is, in fact, one of the recommendations of the NCPP. With respect to air pollution, the project has developed an innovative emissions charge and rebate plan that it recommends be tried in a place where the air quality standards are not now being met. The plan would be implemented at the option of the state and with the approval of EPA. It would replace the individual source emission limits of the State Implementation Plan. None of the charge revenue would accrue to the government. It would be rebated in a way that rewarded producers whose emissions per unit of product were less than the industry average (at the expense of producers whose emissions were greater).

Industry should, upon reflection, find much that is attractive in this plan. It replaces the judgment of government regulators with that of corporate management in arriving at decisions on the appropriate level of pollution reduction for each source. (Charges are set area-wide to produce the acceptable level of total emissions; emissions from each source are not regulated if they are covered by charges.) The plan will produce more reduction in pollution for each dollar spent, because management will act to the point where the unit cost of abatement equals the unit charge. High-cost pollution abatement that is not required to meet the environmental goals will not be necessary.

The proposed plan is attractive to environmentalists because it harnesses the profit motive in support of, rather than in opposition to, the desired public goals. Thus, it is likely to be more effective in achieving those goals.

It will be interesting to see how industry at large responds to this and other marketplace-oriented recommendations of the NCPP.

The private sector does not uniformly embrace the idea of greater emphasis on the marketplace. Some managements probably believe that they can cut a better deal with a human being (even a government regulator!) than with the impersonal forces of the market. Moreover, even if management cannot get a better deal from the human being, they at least have a potential scapegoat for the events that will follow. We have here, in short, both a challenge to and an opportunity for corporate governance.

Is Doing the Minimum a Good Corporate Strategy?

All too often corporate management does the minimum in environmental protection that is required by law. Indeed, where the requirements are expensive or technologically uncertain, even the legal minimum may not be observed.

We can question whether such minimal compliance to maximize profits is even, over the long run, a profit-maximizing strategy. It breeds distrust and opposition and an unwillingness to give an inch for fear the corporation will take a mile.

Where corporations have taken a positive approach, the results have been quite different. An example is Public Service Company of New Mexico, which has tended to move ahead on pollution control more rapidly than their fellow electric utilities. Although they have had problems, their obvious integrity and willingness to respond to environmental and other public concerns has led to unprecedented community support. They have been granted, for example, the privilege of automatic adjustment of rates as their costs (not just their fuel costs!) change. This provision has enabled them to reduce their interest costs. They have been supported by environmental groups in a petition to delay the operation of certain pollution abatement facilities, so as to first obtain more experience with a new technology. They solicited and obtained the agreement of the Sierra Club and New Mexico Citizens for Clean Air and Water not to file suit to prevent the construction and operation of a new power plant; this agreement was helpful to them in financing the plant.

I do not think that corporate managements have been sufficiently aware of the opportunities for enhancing the decision-making environment that could result from a series of concrete actions, not coerced, that respond to public concerns.

Seizing the Opportunity

There is much that corporations and environmental and other citizen groups can now do to enlarge the opening made by the NCPP. The leaders of these organizations, if they agree that a non-adversarial forum can play a useful role in the policy formulation, should voice public support for the processes of the NCPP. They should give careful consideration to the policy recommendations of the NCPP and support them if they agree they have merit. Implementation of the recommendations is the most effective answer to those critics who say that nonadversarial processes are a waste of time.

Consideration should be given to other issues that may yield to a process of joint exploration and policy evaluation. In doing so, it is important to identify and obtain the active involvement of leaders on both sides who have the confidence of their peers and are dedicated to a full exploration of the issues. A neutral institutional setting, such as that provided for the NCPP by Georgetown University's Center for Strategic and International Studies, will probably be needed. Adequate funding must be provided, and those funds needed to cover the costs of individuals from citizen groups should probably be from sources not posing a conflict of interest problem. (Four foundations and three government agencies have contributed to the NCPP for just that reason.)

These and other elements have been important to the progress of the NCPP. It should not be thought, however, that there exists a particular recipe which if religiously followed will lead to inevitable success. In fact, it is important that the participants have a hand in the formulation of the process so that they will be comfortable with and committed to it. In the final analysis, no process will succeed without the good faith and commitment of the participants.

Reginald H. Jones

5

The Relations
between the Board of Directors
and Operating Management

There is a simple and essential point to be made about the current wide-ranging discussion of corporate governance: it is not addressed to a static situation. The very fact of the discussion, coupled with some well-publicized corporate lapses, has had significant impact within many—I would suspect most—of our large enterprises in two ways. First, directors have become more involved, more challenging, and more penetrating in performing board responsibilities. Second, on the intellectual level there has been an effort to develop a theory of the board's role and to define that role in a more systematic way.

Both these responses are healthy. In responding to challenges—some of them well-taken, some not, but all of them inevitable in our current adversary culture—business leadership has to steer a middle course between a reaction which is arrogant or self-righteous on the one side and apologetic or defensive on the other. The important point is to make those improvements in the corporate governance

REGINALD H. JONES *is Chairman and Chief Executive Officer of the General Electric Company. Mr. Jones is also Co-Chairman of the Business Roundtable and of the Labor-Management Group. He is a member of the Advisory Committee for International Monetary Reform and a trustee of the University of Pennsylvania.*

process which failures or malfunctions tell us are required. One of the distinctive virtues of the U.S. business system is its adaptability, its capacity to make mid-course corrections and to respond constructively to new challenges.

The improvements can best be made if they proceed from an overall concept of the place of shareowners, directors, and managers in the corporate decision process. Here the critics have been valuable because they have stimulated a rethinking. The results of this reanalysis appear in recommendations from both chief executives and from the legal profession: statements made in 1978 by the Policy Committee of the Business Roundtable (*The Role and Composition of the Large Publicly Owned Corporations*) and by the Committee on Corporate Laws of the American Bar Association (*Corporate Director's Guidebook*).

Some Proposals for Reform

On the other hand, if one turns from the overall impact of the literature on corporate governance and focuses on particular proposals for change, one finds that some of these proposals are characterized by a sometimes startling lack of familiarity with the realities of the business process, by a reliance on inappropriate analogies from the political arena, and by a naive faith in the sovereign value of organizational mechanics. Before approaching the issues affirmatively, it may help to review some of these proposals.

First, there is the notion that the key concerns about corporate governance can be addressed simply by enlarging the role of audit committees and of the independent public accountants. There is no doubt that the audit process should be rigorous and properly oriented. But as the 1978 report of the Commission on Auditor's Responsibilities makes clear, even the accounting profession sees inherent limits to what auditors and audit committees can accomplish.

The central responsibilities of the audit committee relate to the authenticity of financial statements, to the reliability of underlying records, and to the adequacy of financial controls. Such a committee, with help from the independent public accountants, can deal with financial irregularities, with some disclosure issues, and with conflicts of interest. Even here its efforts need to be based on appropriately framed corporate policies and procedures and to be supported by operating management, by the internal audit function, and by counsel.

However, unless the audit committee is to be transformed into a superboard of directors, there are crucial elements of corporate performance which will be beyond its scope—corporate resource allocation, social or public impacts of corporate activities, compliance with legal and ethical requirements in nonfinancial areas, and some aspects of corporate disclosure obligations. Similarly, these responsibilities will be beyond the proper role and the competence of the independent public accountants.

Second, there is a growing emphasis on establishing an overall board committee structure adapted to the main board responsibilities. This idea is sound so long as it is realized that there is no ideal structure to which all enterprises should be expected to conform in some literal or mechanical way.

A properly designed set of committees can enhance the board's effectiveness and facilitate its work. But the design of the committees and their particular responsibilities will (and should) vary from company to company and reflect in each case the individual tradition, environment, style, and personnel of the enterprise.

For example, one company might combine the functions of management compensation and management selection and succession in one committee. Another might prefer to place responsibility for management selection and succession in a committee responsible also for director succession—a nominating committee. Again, one company might have an executive or operations committee and another might have a committee on corporate strategic plans with similar but not identical responsibilities.

Third, there is a widespread view that it is highly desirable for a board to have a majority of outside directors. The point here, it seems to me, is that in most cases the board should have at least a "critical mass" of outsiders—that is, a number sufficiently large to have a substantial impact on the board decision process. As a 1977 Conference Board report on boards of directors in nine countries confirms, there is an increasing tendency for the boards of large corporations to have a majority of outsiders. But it hardly seems useful to press this notion to the point of engaging in scholastic debates as to whether, for example, a retired officer or a commercial banker is an "outsider."

A more extreme view would exclude all members of management

from the board, except for the chief executive officer. The disadvantages here are obvious: the board loses the benefit of the intimate knowledge of company operations which an "insider" can bring to its deliberations. It also loses the advantage of continuing contact with potential successors to the CEO.

Most of the concerns about "insider" service on the board can be dealt with by measures short of a complete bar to such service. The new Stock Exchange listing requirement excludes management directors from service on an audit committee. It is common practice to exclude "insiders" from any committee considering management compensation and to provide that they shall not constitute a majority of any committee on director succession. In some companies all board committees are chaired by outsiders.

In addition, there are particular issues where nonparticipation by insiders will be appropriate. Depending on the circumstances, this nonparticipation can range from total withdrawal from the meeting to abstention from a vote. If issues of this type constituted a large fraction of the board's business, there would be an argument for a total bar to management directors—but in fact they do not. To the contrary, management directors can make a substantial contribution to most of the matters coming before the board.

Management directors are subject in principle to the same legal constraints as "outsiders." Indeed their responsibilities in a given case may be greater because they may have superior access to the facts. Moreover, any loss of detachment attributable to greater involvement in day-to-day operations will be counter-balanced by greater familiarity with the issues.

Fourth, there are suggestions for separate staffs for boards. The object apparently is to create two channels of communication to the board and some sort of "balance of power" mechanisms to assure that the board is not overly dependent on operating management and particularly on the chief executive officer. Melvin A. Eisenberg thoughtfully summarizes the disadvantages of this proposal in his book on *The Structure of the Corporation*:

> . . . it would create a shadow staff with an institutionalized responsibility to second-guess the management, but with very limited responsibility for results . . . the board's staff could normally be expected only to decide again—with much more limited facilities and feel for the business, and at the price of additional expense and time—issues which management and the corporate staff have already once decided . . .

the proposal would . . . produce a wholly undesirable diffusion of responsibility as among the executives, the shadow staff, the overseeing committee, and the board itself.

As will be developed later in this chapter, there are ways to assure the board's autonomous role without building into our business organizations a bureaucratic adversary process—to the detriment of their competitive efficiency.

Fifth, a closely related notion is that the post of chief executive officer should be separated from that of board chairman. There are cases—reasonably well known in business history—where this has worked well. There are cases, which (for obvious reasons) tend to be less well-publicized, where this system has not worked and where the two consuls have either been at odds or one of them has taken over the dominant role.

The fear in this instance seems to be that the chief executive officer who serves as board chairman is in a position to exercise an unreasonable control over the issues and information going to the board. This overlooks the fact that any prudent CEO will have a strong incentive to develop a relationship of trust with his colleagues on the board and to share with his fellow directors all significant concerns about the enterprise and its future. The risks for a CEO if he fails to earn the confidence of his fellow directors are very high.

Moreover, the CEO, with his day-to-day contact with both line and staff elements of management, is in the best position to assure that the board is addressing the right questions and obtaining the required information. A board chairman not in command of the operating organization is less likely to be fully informed and more likely to miss potential sources of trouble.

In a word, separation of the offices of CEO and board chairman will work if the occupants of the two offices are compatible and collaborate fully and in good faith. But if a CEO is prepared to co-operate with a colleague who is board chairman, he is highly likely to serve the board faithfully in the capacity of chairman. Conversely, the separation of the posts of CEO and chairman will work to the detriment of the board and of the enterprise if a serious rivalry develops between the two incumbents. Experience and common sense tell us to expect this rivalry in a considerable number of cases.

There is one other consideration. In these times one of the inescapable responsibilities of the executive head of the business is to act as a public spokesman and to do so as the principal agent of the board. Anyone other than the executive head will inevitably have less stature and less credibility in the political and public arena. It is rash to suppose that if an enterprise is theoretically or nominally led by two coequal consuls, either one of them will be able to perform as public spokesman on an optimum basis.

Sixth, there are proposals calling for government-appointed directors (mislabeled "public" directors), directors representing employees or labor organizations, and directors representing other nonshareowner constituencies. Fortunately none of these notions commands significant support. It is widely recognized that they are inconsistent with the effective functioning in a competitive market economy of enterprises whose primary function is to furnish goods and services on terms which permit a fair return to investors.

The central principle of the present system is that a director's accountability is to the owners of the enterprise. This accountability includes the obligation to act in the shareowners' long-range interest and, specifically, to act for shareowners in discharging their responsibilities to other groups affected by corporate activities.

If this principle is abandoned, if other corporate constituencies are placed on a plane with shareowners, if directors are required to represent directly the interests of nonshareowner groups, the ultimate consequence will be that directors will be responsible to no one. For in that event there will be no clear measure of directors' responsibility because there will be no clear consensus on primary corporate goals.

Moreover, introducing a variety of noneconomic objectives into the goal structure of U.S. business corporations would call in the long run for a radical shift in current U.S. policies on competition and antitrust, on international trade, on the role of government aid versus private investment, and on the purposes and techniques of corporate regulation.

If the concern is social responsiveness, or "public accountability," the short answer is that in this country at this time, no large corporate enterprise can afford to be perceived as oblivious or contemptuous of matters of genuine social or public concern. These enterprises have to earn from the general public and their political representatives—and earn from year to year—the right to continued existence in their present form and the right to continue to function without radical new governmental constraints.

The responsible business leaders who serve as directors and senior managers of large corporations are acutely aware of this reality. They recognize that the long-range interest of shareowners requires sensitivity to the interests and expectations of other corporate constituencies. Corporations do not have federal "charters," but they do operate under an informal "franchise" from the general public. This franchise is continually under review and can be severely altered or even terminated by public pressure or governmental action.

Seventh, there are proposals for federal legislation establishing standards for directors' conduct. One could better evaluate these proposals if they specified how the proposed federal standards would differ from those now provided in state corporate laws, in the federal securities laws, and in state and federal judicial decisions. Where there have been failures, the cause has not been lack of legal standards, but simple failure to conform to those standards.

If improvement is sought in this area, the focus should be not on the standards, but on the sanctions for their breach. Where a director or officer has profited from a breach of fiduciary obligation, a monetary restitution is eminently appropriate. The situation is different where the charge is neglect rather than conflict of interest. In that situation, an attempt to recover corporate financial losses from a director or officer will be perceived as Draconian.

If it occurred in a major case, one can predict a mass of resignations from corporate boards. In cases of neglect of duty without personal profit, it would be much more realistic to substitute for monetary liability the sanction of suspension from office, including, for a period of time, the right to serve as a director or officer of another publicly-held corporation. (I leave it to the accountants and lawyers to develop the implications of this notion for their own professions.)

Eighth, there are proposals for enlarging shareowner participation in the director nomination process—promoting "shareholder democracy." These proposals run into two obvious and closely related objections. The first is that all the evidence suggests that the overwhelming majority of shareowners have little interest in enhanced participation in corporate affairs. Their interest rather is in dividends and in the market price of their shares. They judge management by financial results and vote primarily by buying and selling shares.

A second and related objection is that new mechanisms for share-owner nomination of directors would, on all present indications, be used primarily by activist minorities interested less in economic performance than in pressing some social or political "cause." Whether the delays, burdens, and inefficiencies incident to these new nomination mechanisms should be imposed involuntarily on the great body of shareowners who do not share the views of the activists presents an interesting philosophical question as to what is meant by "democracy." As the Business Roundtable has suggested, the case is different if the majority of shareowners voluntarily adopt such new procedures rather than having them imposed by a government body.

All these observations have a common theme: many reform proposals, upon analysis, prove to be marginal or simplistic. They underestimate the pressures which already exist to induce responsible corporate conduct, and they assume too readily that changes in formal structure will result in different decisions or behavior. The functioning of corporate boards—like all other human activities—can undoubtedly be improved. But improvement will come incrementally and not through dramatic structural or legal cure-alls.

The Role of Directors

In my judgment, the most important step which can be taken to improve corporate governance is to articulate a clear theory of what the board's job is and of how to go about performing it. This was the objective of the recent year-long project undertaken by the Business Roundtable, an organization composed of chief executive officers of some 185 leading publicly-owned U.S. companies. The project culminated in a Policy Committee paper. The paper attempts to give a concrete and contemporary content to the board's statutory responsibility to "direct the management of" the corporation. The Roundtable Policy Committee defines four core functions for the board of directors:

1. The selection and removal of the chief executive officer and his principal management associates; selection of successor directors; and the development of plans for management and board succession.
2. The consideration of corporate actions and decisions with a potential for major economic impact, including participation in the development of corporate resource allocation decisions ("strategic plans"); and monitoring corporate financial performance.

3. The consideration of significant social impacts of corporate activities and the consideration of views of substantial groups (other than shareowners) significantly affected by such activities.
4. The development of policies and procedures designed to promote, on a sustained and systematic basis, compliance with legal and ethical obligations by all levels of operating management.

The paper goes on to emphasize, as an overriding board responsibility, the establishment (in conjunction with the chief executive officer and his operating and staff colleagues) of systems and procedures designed to assure a timely flow of information to the board.

The premises of these Roundtable prescriptions should be clear. The board will do its job well *if*

1. Its agenda is structured so that it will address the essential issues bearing on how well the corporation is serving shareowners, employees, and others; *and if*
2. The board has mechanisms in place to produce a timely flow of information relevant to the issues it should address.

The words and the underlying ideas are simple enough. It is somewhat like saying that a football team will do well if the players block and tackle well. As in so many other endeavors, everything depends on execution.

This description of the board's role tends initially to provoke reactions from two directions:

1. There are those who suggest that emphasis on the board's crucial responsibility in certain areas tends to denigrate the position of operating management. For example, there is no doubt that the board must select the successor CEO; but it can be countered that one of the primary obligations of an incumbent CEO is to take the lead in identifying, bringing along, and proposing candidates for the succession.

Again, the board should review strategic plans; but these plans, of necessity, must be prepared by the operating organization. Similarly, the board should monitor law compliance; but the initial responsibility is that of managers and their counsel.

All these observations seem to me complementary rather than contradictory. To resort to an analogy, Congressional authority over appropriations is entirely compatible with Executive Branch preparation of an annual budget.

2. Others are eager to reduce the authority of what they perceive to be the "Imperial" Chief Executive Officer. They look for formal rules or constraints designed to limit the power of the CEO and his ability to "dominate" the board.

Some of us who occupy these allegedly "powerful" and "dominating" positions tend to be taken aback by this perception. We feel somewhat like Harry Truman who described the power of his much more exalted office as simply the opportunity to try "to persuade people to do the things they ought to have sense enough to do without my persuading them. . . ."

Operating managers, including CEOs, have no fixed terms of office (except for mandatory retirement provisions in most cases), no equivalent of civil service status, and no equivalent of academic tenure. Operating managers, including CEOs, are regularly turned out of office—as anyone can verify, in spite of euphemistic press releases, by reading the daily business pages.

Important and sensitive relationships such as that between the CEO and the board depend more on the inherent necessities of the situation and on the personality and style of the individuals involved than on any set of formal rules. Let me speak at this point of the necessities of the situation.

If the board is addressing itself to the critical corporate issues and if it is obtaining the right information, it seems unlikely that, in most cases, the board will be unduly influenced by even a very capable and forceful CEO. The legal authority for corporate decision-making rests, after all, in the directors and not in operating management. The legal liabilities and public vulnerabilities of board members make it irrational to resolve issues on any basis except the merits. The tendency to accept recommendations of the CEO will, of course, be strong, provided things are going well. But any unfortunate turn of events—financial or otherwise—will alert the directors and sharpen their inquisitorial instincts.

The other side of the coin is that although a political system can tolerate for long periods an adversary relationship and severe tension among its various branches, a business organization cannot. If a board and a CEO have continuing differences on a number of significant corporate matters, then the answer is unavoidable—the CEO will have to go.

Keeping Directors Informed

Of course, my assumption in all the foregoing is that the board is obtaining the relevant information. I recognize that this assumption is critical. If one wishes to assure that the board is performing effectively, this is where the focus should be. Without good information, changes in board structure or composition won't help.

A central premise of this chapter is that the sanctions already applicable to directors and to senior managers—liability in derivative or class action suits; liability, criminal and civil, under regulatory statutes; and the risk of public opprobrium—are a strong deterrent to questionable or improper behavior. These sanctions make it highly likely that a corporation will be properly managed if the right issues are presented to the board along with the information required to resolve those issues.

It follows that the director's key job is to take whatever steps are necessary to provide reasonable confidence that management is presenting the right questions for board consideration, that the board agendas are on target, and that the board is receiving relevant information on a timely basis. In corporate governance, the reliance of shareowners and of others affected must be on the effective performance of this directorial obligation.

The great challenge then is: what mechanisms, what arrangements should the board prescribe in order to provide reasonable assurance that it will receive relevant information in time?

Experience suggests that the most effective approach is to open channels of communication between the board on the one side and operating personnel, both line and staff, on the other. The required knowledge is usually somewhere in the organization. The problem is to get it to the board.

This means that the board should receive regular reports from key members of line management. It should receive regular reports as well from staff officers, such as the senior financial officer and the General Counsel, covering their respective areas of responsibility. The CEO should participate in this reporting process but should not function as a censor.

Reports from line officers should cover long-range forecasts, strategic plans, and problem areas for major sectors of the corporation's business. Reports from staff officers should cover sensitive topics such as equal employment opportunity, health and safety of employees, and environmental effects of company operations and company products.

Obviously this enumeration is intended to be illustrative rather than exhaustive. The persons making the reports, the timing of the reports, and their focus will shift from time to time with changes in the business or in the external environment or in public expectations.

It is clearly in management's self-interest, in the normal case, to assure a proper flow of information to the board. The directors are the bosses of the enterprise, with the power to fire as well as hire. Rule One in any such relationship is: don't surprise the boss.

There is always the danger of aberrations. But the risk of aberration is drastically reduced if directors act on their obligation to inquire where there is any reason to believe that the board is not being adequately informed. At least in my own observation, and contrary to some of the literature, directors do not hesitate to make such inquiries.

These underlying realities of the board-management relationship can be reenforced by a set of board-approved policies covering management conduct in sensitive areas, such as antitrust. These policies should provide for periodic reporting to the board. Such policies and reporting procedures are powerful tools to assist the board in its monitoring function.

Although it is impractical and unwise to attempt to develop a universal or inflexible set of rules or mechanisms for communications to the board, the underlying objective should be determined by a "surprise test." Ideally the board should never be surprised by a substantial corporate mishap or corporate problem, business, social, or legal. One hundred percent performance against this criterion is probably not attainable in this demanding and imperfect world; but any case where the board is surprised should be regarded as a management failure.

Improvements in Board Performance

Some who have followed the discussion to this point may say: "Very well, if the main problem is to see to it that the directors are informed, how can shareowners and the general public have confidence that this will in fact happen?" It is not enough to say that it will happen in a well-run corporation. Not all corporations will be well run.

If one seeks a perfect world, or absolute assurance that everything will always be done right, I know of no answer to this question. For those who look at the subject bearing in mind that the perfect is the enemy of the good, I would suggest three answers.

1. Except for the observation about different sanctions made above, I know of no concrete proposal for new legislation, which goes beyond present rules as to director responsibility in state corporate laws and in the federal securities laws, to address this problem in a sensible and useful way. There are, of course, suggestions from some quarters that private business corporations should be restructured on government bureaucratic models. Apart from their transparent deficiencies, these suggestions are motivated by the same ideology which has already brought us so much counter-productive regulation. Thoughtful observers believe that the growing web of federal controls is making our economy more arthritic and less venturesome, and that the challenge is to make these controls lighter, not more ponderous.

2. We should not let the fact that philosophizing on corporate governance is very much a growth industry blind us to the reality that boards of directors—to an extent because of some well-publicized recent failures—are functioning more aggressively and more critically. It is appropriate to challenge corporate leadership—directors and managers—to do better. But it is also proper to acknowledge that there has been a response and that corporate leadership *is* doing better. The Conference Board studies corroborate this assessment.

3. One must attach considerable significance to the adoption by the Business Roundtable of its policy statement on the role and composition of the board of directors. That document has a dual function. It is a statement of position on corporate governance—a contribution to the current debate—addressed to the general public, Congress and governmental agencies, the investment community, and interested academics, among others. It is also a reformist document addressed to U.S. corporate leadership. By setting standards for effective board performance, it should lead to critical self-examination in many companies and should reenforce other current pressures for reform and improvement.

Another significant development which should have the same effect is the Corporate Director's Guidebook issued by the Committee on Corporate Laws of the American Bar Association. This guide-book, by also setting standards for director conduct (broadly compatible with those of the Roundtable), should rally the considerable influence of the corporate bar (inside general counsel and outside law firms) in support of revised and more effective board procedures.

Primary Task of the Board: Cooperative versus Adversary Relationships

I should not close without returning to the theme of some observations I have made elsewhere on this general subject of corporate governance.

Much of the literature preoccupied with creating a better balance of power between operating management and the board overlooks the simple reality that if they are not mutually supportive, the effectiveness of the enterprise in a competitive marketplace will suffer. The right investments will not be made in time, the right ventures will not be undertaken, necessary corrective measures will not be taken, timely decisions to abandon unprofitable lines will not be made, morale will suffer, good people will be lost.

For the iron law of competition is that a business organization must have clear goals, a responsive and flexible decision process, and cohesiveness in operation. There is room for free expression of differences, for candor, and for disagreement on specific issues. But there is no room for bureaucratic delays, for factionalism, or for prolonged adversary relationships. This is true all the way up the line from the lowest level of operating management to the board-CEO interface.

I have identified some elements of an effective business decision process:

1. decentralization of initiative and decision-making to the level of management which must deal directly with the problem and which has the best access to the facts;
2. communications which are quick, informal, and candid;
3. clear lines of authority to resolve differences;
4. separate channels of communication to top management from staff and line elements of the organization; and
5. strong leadership to select, assign and motivate people, to set overall standards and directions, and to resolve conflicts within the organization.

These are the requirements for successful operation of a business enterprise in a competitive market economy. The broad discretion which boards of directors typically entrust to operating management and to the CEO reflects these requirements and not laxity or inadvertence or misunderstanding.

Today, U.S. society is making—it must make—enormous demands on the private sector, and notably on that portion of the private sector composed of large publicly-owned corporations. These demands are for massive new investments (with inevitable risks); for constantly expanding employment opportunities (particularly for women and minorities); for innovative technologies responsive to energy and environmental concerns; for improved productivity to combat inflation; for effective competitive performance in international trade and investment against the formidable multinational enterprises based in Western Europe and Japan; and for support of public and governmental objectives in other areas.

If the business community is to respond to these demands, it must rely on its traditional strengths—on initiative, resourcefulness, innovativeness, flexibility. These requirements in turn dictate a process and structure of corporate governance where the emphasis must be on cooperation between directors and operating management, and not on formalized adversary relationships. The primary task of the board should be viewed not as negative and restrictive, but as positive and liberating, designed to bring forth the full productive potential of the business corporation.

Lee J. Seidler

6

Auditing and Social Control

> *Accounting and control—that is the* main *thing required for "arranging" the smooth working, the correct functioning of the first phase of communist society.*
>
> *All citizens are transformed here into hired employees of a* single *nationwide state "syndicate." All that is required is that they should work equally, do their proper share of work, and get equally paid.*
>
> *The accounting and control necessary for this have been* simplified *by capitalism to the extreme and reduced to the extraordinarily simple operations. . . .*
>
> *When the* majority *of the people begin independently and everywhere to keep such accounts and maintain such control over the capitalists (now converted into employees) and over the intellectual gentry who preserve their capitalist habits, this control will really become universal, general, popular; and there will be no way of getting away from it, there will be "nowhere to go."*
>
> V. I. Lenin
The State and the Revolution (1917)

LEE J. SEIDLER, *Professor of Accounting at New York University, is Presiding Member of the AICPA Commission on Auditors' Responsibilities and a Director of the National Association of Accountants for the Public Interest. Author of numerous articles on auditors' responsibilities and of the recently published (and well received) book* Social Accounting, *Professor Seidler is also Vice President of The Shubert Foundation.*

American accounting traditionally has been viewed as having two principal functions:

1. helping to assure the security of the corporate assets, and
2. measuring the returns obtained by corporate management from the assets.

The need to fulfill these two assumed functions of accounting—stewardship and performance measurement—has guided the formation of accounting principles in the United States.

Consider, however, the preceding comments of one of the founders of communism. Lenin did not view accounting as a means of making it more difficult for capitalists to pilfer the assets of the state. Nor was he considering the necessity to evaluate the performance of different enterprises in order to achieve maximum efficiency in the communist economy. Neither stewardship nor performance measurement for Lenin; to him the simple double entry bookkeeping device was a way to make people do what they were supposed to. Accounting *is* control.

Of course, the idea that accounting may be used as a device for control is neither new nor unfamiliar to us. Early nineteenth century American accountants led the world in the development of cost accounting systems intended to control manufacturing operations. Today, sophisticated management accounting systems control not only routine production activities, but also the delivery of services and complex ventures, such as the design and development of nuclear submarines.

In a modern adaptation of Lenin's ideas, New York University offers a course titled "Internal Reporting and Control" which focuses on the theory and application of accounting techniques to provide better control both for and of management. At the Harvard Business School the quaintly archaic sound of the title "Accounting" has been scrapped entirely, in favor of a department which teaches "Control."

Thus, while it is traditional to consider American accounting a device used to protect the interests and to improve the decision-making processes of investors and creditors, we have long since recognized the potential of accounting as a control measure in much the same terms as Lenin.

The theme of this book is corporate governance. The word "governance" sometimes carries a more benign image than "control."

We tend to associate the term "self-governance" with the word "governance," while "control" implies the imposition of outside power. The dictionary does not really agree. Governance is also the exercise of authority. Looking at public corporations, people are deeply concerned about authority; who holds it and how it is exercised.

When we speak of accounting, we are dealing with a device for governance—or control. This chapter deals with the use and abuse of accounting as a device for control and governance of the corporation.

Conventional Accounting as a Control Device

The application of accounting to the traditional problems of stewardship and performance actually involves a strong element of control. Using accounting as a stewardship device to assure reasonable security of assets was an early application. Fifteenth century Venetian merchants used the double entry bookkeeping system to define the results of their trading ventures. A Venetian monk described their techniques in 1494 in the world's first accounting text. At its peak, the Ottoman Empire stretched from the gates of Vienna to the tip of the Arabian peninsula. An elaborate system of accounting stipulated the tax revenues which were due from every corner of the Empire and assured that the Sultan received the right amount on the right date. In seventeenth century England, as nobles tired of the rustic life and moved to take up residence in the wicked cities, the development of accounting systems was commissioned to provide them with some assurance that their stewards, still managing the manors, were kept reasonably honest. Thus the introduction of the term "stewardship" in the English language accounting vocabulary.

All of these examples involve the use of accounting by one party to control the actions of another. In most cases, it is an owner attempting to gain assurance about the activities of a hired manager, subordinate, or subject. The second traditional application of accounting principles, performance measurement, is merely a more sophisticated version of accounting used for stewardship purposes. As enterprises grew larger, concern with pilferage of the assets diminished and was replaced by a desire to obtain maximum performance from paid managers. Accounting evolved accordingly, and the dominant concern with assets and liabilities gave way to a growing interest in measuring performance, particularly as expressed in terms of net income.

When accounting measures performance it is usually an indirect means of control. The manager of an enterprise makes certain decisions or takes actions; then accounting attempts to measure the results. Someone else—a superior, an owner, or a potential owner —then makes decisions regarding the enterprise and the manager. Traditional accounting suggests that the most frequent situation is that of an owner or creditor determining what actions to take relative to an investment or loan. More recently, greater attention has been accorded to the decision processes of *potential* investors and creditors. Indeed, the Securities Act of 1933, which focuses on registration statements and initial offerings of shares, is almost completely occupied with the interests of potential investors and creditors in measuring the performance of the enterprise.

Control of the Accounting System

Heisenberg's principle of indeterminacy stipulates the relationship between an observer and a phenomenon under observation: the item being measured will always be affected by the measurement process. The same considerations apply to accounting. When in the 1960s investors and potential investors began to pay more attention to measuring certain dimensions of "performance," managers attempted to deliver that performance whether or not it existed. If investors desired rapidly growing income, accounting principles and practices were bent to provide the desired picture. For example, the recognition of revenue was accelerated in industries such as leasing, franchising, and land sales.

The idea that a manager whose performance is being measured by accounting will attempt to distort the measurement to favor himself was not new to those who were using accounting to measure performance of units *within* corporations. Managers learned long ago that judicious negotiation over matters such as intercompany transfer prices and corporate overhead allocations could have a more profound impact than hard work on their measured performance.

When a group sees that their performance is being measured by accounting and that actions affecting their interests will be taken by those using the performance measurement, they will attempt to influence the accounting system itself. If an accounting system is used as a control, control of the accounting system becomes desirable. As William Werntz, former chief accountant of the SEC noted in the 1940s:

> Business accounting, for purposes of internal control of personnel, costs and policies and for reporting to inactive owners, has largely developed in the United States within the last half-century. It was impossible that this development of accounting as a control device originating in the business world would go unnoticed by legislative bodies and judicial and administrative officials. It was inevitable that, in the search for effective means of obtaining data about social and economic phenomena, resort should quickly be had to accounting data. Thenceforth it was but a short and logical step to reliance on the accounting process, first as a means of regularly observing the activities of economic units, and then as a means of prescribing and proscribing courses of action.

OIL AND GAS ACCOUNTING AS AN EXAMPLE

Werntz's comment was made many years ago, but it seems clear that its spirit was recalled by Congress when it formulated the Energy Production and Conservation Act of 1975 (PL 94-385). The law stipulates that the Department of Energy's National Energy Information System should contain "such energy information as is necessary to carry out the Federal Energy Administration's statistical and forecasting activities."

If resources are sufficient, it should also include information to "define the institutional structure of the energy supply system and permit analysis of this structure and of energy resource production, distribution and consumption in the short and long runs."

Cutting through the jargon, it seems reasonably clear that the National Energy Information System will be used to regulate and control the structure of the energy supply of the United States. However, Congress understood, or was advised, that the accounting systems used by the oil and gas companies were frequently inconsistent. The largest oil and gas companies use variations of a method known as "successful efforts" accounting. Many more, generally smaller, companies use a method called "full cost" accounting. The two systems provide sharply differing measures of performance. Since a data base requires a degree of uniformity, Congress included in the 1975 Energy Act a requirement that the Securities and Exchange Commission develop a uniform method of accounting for oil and gas companies.

FORMULATION OF ACCOUNTING STANDARDS

Since the late 1930s, the SEC, by delegating the actual formulation of the principles to a professional organization in the private sector, has exercised its statutory authority over the accounting principles and practices of companies whose shares are publicly traded. The task of developing accounting principles was first entrusted to the American Institute of Certified Public Accountants (AICPA) but now rests with the Financial Accounting Standards Board (FASB). As the principles are developed by the private body, the SEC informally reviews them and decides whether they are accceptable for Commission purposes. Except in rare instances, this consultation and coordination has generally resulted in the Commission's accepting practices developed in the private sector.

In connection with the Energy Act of 1975, the Commission wished to continue this relationship. It prevailed on Congress to amend the original version of the bill to allow the SEC to "subcontract" the formulation of uniform accounting principles for oil and gas companies to the FASB. As a result, the FASB developed, with some haste, Statement of Financial Accounting Standards (SFAS) No. 19. As might have been expected, the companies affected by SFAS No. 19 were too powerful and too diverse to permit the Board to develop a standard which would be reasonably acceptable to all parties concerned. As a result, when it was issued, SFAS No. 19 faced a highly-organized, well-financed campaign aimed at its overthrow.

The campaign against SFAS No. 19 involves a labyrinth of contrasting goals and interests which is difficult to dissect completely. However, several of the principal elements of the controversy are reasonably clear and relate to the issue of accounting as a key device in corporate governance.

THE DEBATE

A brief digression into the complexity of oil and gas accounting, and particularly of the accounting associated with exploration efforts, is required at this point. As a practical matter, while there is some disparity among companies because of their size, inclinations, and circumstances, most accounting practices in the oil and gas industry are relatively comparable, except for those associated with exploratory activities.

As noted earlier, all of the "majors" account for their exploration activities using a method called "successful efforts." Under successful efforts accounting, only the costs directly associated with successful efforts, that is the cost of wells which actually result in the discovery of economically recoverable reserves, are capitalized in the balance sheet of the company. Other costs of exploration, most of which are appropriately termed "dry-hole" costs, are immediately expensed. Since about eight out of ten exploratory wells are unsuccessful, under the successful efforts method most of the costs of exploration are immediately charged to expense and thus serve to reduce profit. On the other hand, while the *cost* of the successful wells is shown as an asset in the company's balance sheet, no recognition is given to their *value*, which is obviously far higher.

Under the alternative full cost method, *all* costs of exploration, whether they result in success or failure, are capitalized as assets in the balance sheet. These costs are subsequently amortized on a proportionate basis against the revenues from the oil pumped from the successful wells. Full cost accounting is used by the majority of smaller oil companies where exploration accounts for a much larger proportion of total operations than in the case of the vertically integrated majors. During the period preceding the issuance of SFAS No. 19, companies using each method asked the FASB either to adopt only their method or to permit the continued use of alternatives. The latter option, however, was precluded by the Congressional mandate to develop a uniform system of accounting. When SFAS No. 19 was issued, it adopted the successful efforts method and prohibited the use of full cost accounting. As might be expected, the companies which had already adopted successful efforts accounting on a voluntary basis were content with the outcome and retired from the fray.

Concerted action before issuance and discontent after issuance of new accounting pronouncements is not unique. The FASB's effort to change bank accounting for restructured debt was met with great and effective resistance before it was issued, and the FASB acquiesced in the position taken by the banks. Acquiescence did not bring peace, for SFAS No. 8 was greeted with a flood of complaints after it was issued and continues to be contentious. In previous cases, the disgruntled parties contented themselves with a good deal of grumbling but no overt action. In this case, however, the unsatisfactory pronouncement was greeted by intensified lobbying efforts.

Most of the full cost companies immediately lamented the adoption of successful efforts. However, many companies also recomputed their results utilizing the new standard, and some found, to their considerable surprise, that while absolute reported profit levels were lowered, the all important growth curve of earnings was steeper. Companies with this unexpected bonus were inclined to retire from the controversy. However, these defections left a substantial number of smaller oil and gas companies who still perceived SFAS No. 19 to be inimicable to their interests. In particular, they feared that the sharply reduced profits they would report under SFAS No. 19 would no longer allow them to finance their operations. These small oil exploration companies were joined by several substantially larger enterprises, such as International Paper, which had recently entered the oil and gas business as a means of obtaining a secondary return on their large land holdings. Such companies were almost certain to have negative results from the application of SFAS No. 19, and they strongly preferred full cost accounting.

In addition, the managements of many oil companies believed that mandated uniform accounting is a prelude to governmental efforts to regulate the oil and gas industry on a rate of return basis. Successful efforts, which tends to reduce reported profits, would be attractive as regulatory accounting for the larger companies. However, successful efforts accounting would virtually wipe out the capital accounts of many smaller companies. Rates of return computed on nonexistent invested capital amounts are less than attractive. The smaller companies perceived that full cost would provide them with a less vulnerable situation under regulation.

BRINGING THE GOVERNMENT INTO THE BATTLE

Since the new accounting required under SFAS No. 19 was originally mandated by the government, those opposed to SFAS No. 19 focused their efforts not on the apparently immovable FASB, but rather on the government of the United States.

Opponents argued that for many companies SFAS No. 19 would cause losses and that the combination of reduced profits and shrunken asset bases would make it more difficult for the full cost, and usually smaller, companies to raise capital. This contention, which remains unproved, suggests that the larger successful efforts companies would have an undue competitive advantage over the smaller oil and gas companies. This is an argument obviously calculated to appeal to the Department of Justice, and it did. On February 27, 1978, the Department of Justice called on the Securities and Exchange Commission to postpone the implementation of SFAS No. 19 on the grounds that successful efforts accounting was not sufficiently better than full cost to justify the potential anticompetitive impacts of the adoption of the former method.

Appeals were made to members of Congress on similar grounds. Senators Haskell and Bartlett introduced an amendment in conference committee to the then pending energy bill stipulating that Congress had not intended in the 1975 Act to regulate the public financial reporting of the oil and gas companies. This amendment was eventually rejected by the committee.

Since the uniform accounting required by SFAS No. 19 was to be used in the Department of Energy's information data base, the Department should have had an interest in the nature of the information. The Department of Energy indicated it would make a recommendation to the SEC regarding SFAS No. 19 but not until it held hearings. On February 21 and 22, 1978, more than forty parties, including this writer, testified at Department of Energy hearings held in Washington, D.C. As might be expected, the chairman of the Financial Accounting Standards Board appeared to defend SFAS No. 19, but most of the commentators were opposed to the FASB pronouncement. The Securities and Exchange Commission hearings on the issue were scheduled to begin in late March 1978. By the end of February almost one hundred parties had indicated their desire to testify in the Washington portion of the hearings. Another fifty indicated that they would appear at separate hearings to be held in Houston.

In one sense it is reassuring that when a significant number of Americans, be they oil companies or a persecuted minority, are dissatisfied with their treatment, they have the right to attempt to obtain redress from the government. In a more narrow sense, however, there are ominous portents in these activities and in the competition to play one government unit against another to win the battle.

The kinds of actions now being taken to influence oil and gas accounting threaten to destroy an unusual private sector-government partnership which has worked reasonably well for decades. Corporate financial reporting practices have influenced the governance of the corporation. Periodic financial statements, audited by independent public accountants, have provided a substantial measure of confidence to investors and creditors that their funds can be entrusted, with reasonable security, to the management of the corporation. Conscientious application of generally accepted accounting principles in the preparation of financial statements, again aided by the efforts of independent auditors, has provided useful measures of corporate performance and a basis for rational decision-making by informed investors and creditors. The quality of audited financial statements and the image they convey of a corporation have had great influence over the ability to raise money and thus have governed the mobilization and flow of enormous amounts of capital into business enterprise.

If the compromise is upset, government influence over accounting will be greatly increased.

The SEC's Role in Forming Accounting Principles

The development of accounting principles has involved a cooperative efforts between private sector organizations and a government regulatory agency, the Securities and Exchange Commission.

The SEC has statutory power under Section 19(a) of the 1933 Act to:

> prescribe the form . . . in which required [accounting] information shall be set forth, the items or details to be shown in the balance sheet and earning statement, and the methods to be followed in the preparation of the accounts. . . .

This grant of power is clearly broad enough to permit the SEC to prescribe completely the accounting of companies whose shares are publicly held. However, in Accounting Series Release No. 4 (1938), the SEC indicated its support for generally accepted accounting principles defined by the private sector and set the pattern for the system of "codetermination" which presently exists.

Those not directly involved in the process of forming accounting principles and auditing standards often do not appreciate the degree to which the SEC does affect the development of specific pronouncements. Through the Office of the Chief Accountant, the Commission indicates which accounting or auditing problems it considers most pressing. In some cases, such as in disclosure of profits arising on the early retirement of debt, the Commission has virtually dictated immediate action by the FASB. More often, however, the Commission suggests its areas of interest informally or approves the topics being considered by the private bodies. As pronouncements are formulated by the FASB or the AICPA, drafts are reviewed in detail with members of the Commission staff, whose views receive high priority. Generally speaking, pronouncements are not issued without the blessing of the SEC staff.

There are few departures from this pattern. After receiving considerable pressure from the Kennedy administration, the SEC overruled the Accounting Principles Board on accounting for the benefits of the original investment tax credit. The requirement for supplementary disclosure of replacement cost information (ASR No. 190) was promulgated unilaterally by the SEC. The Commission rationalized this departure from the usual path of consultation by calling replacement cost a disclosure, rather than an accounting requirement.

Consultation between the private sector and government does not end with the formulation of accounting principles. Regardless of the specificity of accounting pronouncements—and they have tended to grow more detailed—questions of interpretation abound. In theory, such questions are resolved by consultation between a company's management and its independent auditors. In practice, both parties will frequently journey to Washington to obtain SEC staff sanction for a particular interpretation. In such cases, the SEC staff tends to place both reliance and obligations on the independent auditor. The staff will not always accept an accounting interpretation which has been agreed to by both management and the independent auditor, but it will almost never approve accounting which is not proposed, or at least accepted, by the independent auditor.

Some observers believe that this system ought to be a prototype for private sector-government relationships. Certainly, it closely resembles the cooperation between the government of Japan and Japanese corporations, a pattern many have praised.

Other observers are less enamored with the system. Robert Chatov argues that the SEC has failed to follow its statutory mandate. The staff of the Senate Subcommittee on Reports, Accounting, and Man-

agement took essentially the same position in its report "The Accounting Establishment" (The Metcalf Report) and suggested that
some other government agency might be required to establish accounting principles and practices. A somewhat milder view was
taken by the House Subcommittee on Oversight and Investigations
(the Moss subcommittee) which urged the SEC to assume direct responsibility for development of a framework for accounting and
financial reporting.

(However, in a subsequent report, signed by the members of the
subcommittee rather than the staff, the Metcalf committee took
cognizance of progress being made by the private sector and did
not repeat many of the demands of the earlier staff document.)

Thus, there has been no shortage of recent attacks on the present
system of establishing accounting principles and practices which
govern corporate financial reporting.

Now, with respect to a particular pronouncement (SFAS No. 19)
dissenters have moved beyond the procedures available to them
during the private sector formulation process and have asked several
government agencies and members of Congress to reverse the decision of the Financial Accounting Standards Board. At this writing
the matter has not been resolved. If they are successful, it is difficult
to believe that this will not be taken as a signal to other groups
dissatisfied with accounting and financial reporting rules. It is not
unreasonable to believe that any industry possessed of reasonable
determination and wealth will henceforth journey to Washington
to seek redress for its accounting grievances. The result would inevitably be an increase in the influence of government on the development of accounting principles and a corresponding decrease
in the independence, influence, and viability of the Financial Accounting Standards Board. The Board will become a mere puppet
of the government and perhaps eventually be replaced by a government agency.

Would such a change necessarily be bad? I believe it would. While
the government of the United States is the greatest engine for the
exercise of mass democracy in the history of mankind, it has not
demonstrated any significant capability in the accounting area. To
the contrary, accounting practices prescribed by the government,
such as the requirements of the Interstate Commerce Commission,
have frequently proved to be disastrous for the industries affected

by them. There is general agreement that the depreciation practices of the railroads, under methods sanctioned by the ICC, must bear a significant portion of the responsibility for the present sad state of the American railroad system. Similar examples abound in contrast to a paucity of demonstrations of government accounting competence.

Equally critical to the issue of corporate governance is the question of how the government might use control of accounting for its purposes. I have enough faith in the strength in American democratic institutions to overcome any fear that the United States government would follow Lenin down the path of using accounting as a means of total control over the actions of the citizenry. However, several previous experiences with government legislated accounting principles are not reassuring. In 1962, for example, at the recommendation of President Kennedy, Congress enacted the Investment Tax Credit as a device to stimulate a sagging economy. The Investment Tax Credit produced a tax benefit which had to be reflected in the financial statements of corporations. Most accountants believed that the benefit should be related to the use of the assets whose purchase gave rise to the credit. Hence, the accounting profession, acting through the then authoritative body, the Accounting Principles Board, issued APB Opinion No. 2, which required that the investment tax credit be amortized over the life of the related assets.

The Kennedy administration, however, believed that greater economic stimulation would result if the full benefit of the Investment Tax Credit were immediately recognized in corporate income statements, thus causing substantial rises in reported profits. With this in mind, the administration, through the Treasury Department, placed substantial pressure on the Securities and Exchange Commission to reject APB Opinion No. 2. The SEC did so, with the result that the APB issued its Opinion No. 4 shortly thereafter, which also permitted the "flow through" method favored by the Kennedy administration.

In 1971, the Investment Tax Credit was reenacted. Accountants appear to have short political memories and, unfortunately, the same scenario was repeated. This time Congress took the initiative and included in the Revenue Act of 1971 a provision which prohibited accountants from requiring anyone to account for the Investment Tax Credit in any particular manner. As one U.S. Senator remarked, "When I want to inflate the American economy, no bunch of bookkeepers is going to stop me."

Thus, there is good reason to suspect that increased government involvement with corporate financial reporting practices would lead, as Mr. Werntz predicted, to the government's "prescribing and proscribing courses of action." We have seen this in another significant area, generally referred to as illegal or questionable payments, which has greatly preoccupied both the business community and the government in recent years.

Concern with Illegal and Questionable Payments

The origin of this preoccupation with illegal and questionable activities is not entirely clear. I would venture to guess that it derives from the Watergate scandal and the actions and revelations which followed it. Although some misconduct on the part of corporations was disclosed by the Department of Justice and the Special Prosecutor, the staff of the Securities and Exchange Commission was largely left out of the action.

Shortly after the resignation of President Nixon, the SEC began to press for the disclosure of corporate activities loosely defined as "illegal and questionable payments." The Commission has argued that while the amounts in most cases have been insignificant on any absolute financial scale, the nature of the items disclosed and their implications for management integrity and reliability of the corporation's system of internal control would be material to many investors. This "qualitative" concept of materiality would be accepted by many accountants and is quite difficult to argue with. Nevertheless, the SEC's contention that in the area of illegal and questionable actions it is merely requiring the disclosure of material financial information and not attempting to control corporate actions must be taken with some skepticism.

It seems obvious that the disclosure of illegal actions will lead to some form of punishment. Thus, by requiring disclosure of illegal and questionable payments, the SEC was, in fact, forbidding them and placing itself in a position of regulating corporate conduct. Accounting and financial reporting have thus been harnessed by the Securities and Exchange Commission to function as a vehicle for supposedly introducing a higher standard of corporate morality.

This in turn leads to another aspect of the relationship between accounting and the governance of the corporation. We have thus far discussed this issue in the context of accounting principles and the control of their development. There is another key issue: whether accountants actually have the ability to apply the rules in such a way as to actually control corporate actions.

Lenin, in the quote at the start of this chapter, was quite sanguine about the ability of accounting and accountants to accomplish his purposes:

> The accounting and control necessary for this have been simplified by capitalism to the extreme and reduced to the extraordinarily simple operations—which any literate person can perform—of supervising and recording, knowledge of the four rules of arithmetic, and issuing appropriate receipts.

One need not attempt the trial of the CPA examination to understand that Lenin vastly oversimplified the problems associated with accounting and management. Accounting has always been a complex field, but its complexity has frequently been masked by the willingness of accountants to accept the imposition of simplifying conventions. For example, the extremely complex problem of providing for the wearing out of the corporate productive assets is reduced to a mere arithmetic problem by the accounting convention that fixed assets be carried at cost. The cost is charged to income over the estimated life of the asset under some simple formula, such as straight line or declining balance depreciation. The actual measurement of asset expiration is almost impossible, but accounting conventions tend to make it appear simple. These ideas have prevailed with little change since the enactment of the Sixteenth Amendment to the Constitution (the federal income tax). However, the accelerated rate of inflation of the mid-1970s has forced accountants to new levels of complexity in valuing assets, thus far with no great degree of success.

The concern with illegal and questionable corporate payments provides a similar case of a new and expanded demand on accounting technology, one which is integral to corporate governance.

The first stage of the SEC's preoccupation was a "voluntary" program under which corporations were encouraged to conduct internal investigations to determine whether they had made illegal or questionable payments and to disclose the results. Under the voluntary program, it was generally understood that corporations which cooperated by investigating and disclosing would not be the subject of additional Commission sanctions.

Initial experiences with the voluntary program disclosed a basic problem: actually finding concealed illegal or questionable payments could be quite difficult. In many cases corporate executives had made such payments under the assumption that they were tacitly permitted. In such instances, often only minimal attempts were made at concealment. That is, payments were debited to expense accounts such as "Commissions paid," rather than to "Bribes," and they were not difficult to find.

However, if reasonable efforts were made to conceal payments and the affected executives did not volunteer to disclose their misconduct, auditors searching for the activities encountered great difficulties. If bribes were buried in legal or consulting fees and directed to recipients through third parties, they could only be found after intensive investigation, if at all.

The image of the implacable auditor, ferreting out a concealed fraud, is well entrenched in the popular literature. The image, however, is not in accord with reality. Auditors are accountants by training and profession. They are neither lawyers nor detectives. Their education is concerned with comprehension of accounting theory, for financial reporting purposes and for management controls, but not with techniques of investigation and interrogation. In this respect, it is interesting to note that the auditors who were called in to examine Equity Funding Corporation of America *after* the revelation of the fraud found it extremely difficult to reconstruct accurate books of account. The work required interrogation of those involved in the fraud. The auditors found themselves untrained for such work and heavily dependent on lawyers.

It was not only hard to find concealed illegal payments, but it was also hard to decide if certain payments were, in fact, illegal. An auditor's accounting training, along with his total education, is adequate to enable him to determine that a cash payment made to an American customs official is illegal. An accountant's training, however, does not include lessons on the legality of political contributions made by individuals and corporations at the state, federal, and local level. Nor does it equip him to determine whether or not it is illegal to pay a sales commission to an Indonesian government official. Thus, auditors are frequently not in a position to determine whether or not they should be concerned with many of the questionable items they might have discovered.

The lack of ability of accountants to find and judge illegal and questionable acts was compounded by another factor: the inability of corporate top management to exercise control over their subordinates. As noted earlier, the compensation and advancement of executives frequently depend heavily on divisional profit levels. If operating managers believe that the profit levels of their divisions depend on the payment of bribes, they will tend to continue the practice. The controller of a large multinational corporation related (during testimony at a Congressional hearing) the problem of a particular foreign unit of his company. Auditors had detected and reported illegal bribes being paid by the manager of a foreign subsidiary. Top management gave orders that the practice be stopped.

The manager of the subsidiary agreed, but actually continued the practice. Subsequent examination by the auditors indicated the continuation, and the same scenario was repeated. Not until the subsidiary's manager was replaced was the parent corporation able to end the illegal payments.

This incident suggests another problem in the illegal payments area. The principal device for prevention of such payments is the corporate control system. Internal controls can be established which have as their goal the prevention of unauthorized illegal payments. However, no control system has yet been designed which cannot be overridden by the highest level administrator of an autonomous business unit. If the manager of the subsidiary wants to make illegal payments, he cannot be restrained by a control system. Only subsequent detection, or the threat of subsequent detection by auditors, will have any success. With the knowledge of limits to the detective powers of auditors, managers can afford to be bold in subverting controls.

Note, too, that the earlier references were to auditors engaged to make special examinations to find illegal payments in connection with the SEC's voluntary program. These one-time examinations were conducted in great detail and were expensive. The work involved would not have been comprehended in normal audits. If it were to be included in conventional audits—and if line manage-

ment made greater efforts to conceal payments—the cost of the
normal audit would increase significantly, while the possibilities of
detection would decline.

The obvious problems associated with the prevention and detection of illegal and questionable payments did not dampen the enthusiasm of those who believe that American corporations should
not be permitted to engage in bribery and similar acts in any country. In January 1977, the SEC issued Securities Exchange Act Release No. 34-13185, which bears the impressive title, "Promotion
of the Reliability of Financial Information, Prevention of the Concealment of Questionable or Illegal Corporate Payments and Practices and Disclosure of the Involvement of Management in Specified
Types of Transactions."

The SEC has no direct authority over corporate actions unrelated
to securities markets. However, as cited earlier, it does have the
authority to compel companies whose shares are publicly traded to
keep accurate books and records, and it has considerable power over
disclosure practices. The Commission followed the simple expedient
of suggesting that all transactions, including those that are illegal
or questionable, should be reflected accurately in the accounting
records. Material financial information should, of course, be disclosed, and the SEC made the illegal payments material by fiat.

Thus, the Commission proposed that issuers should record bribes
not as "Commissions" or "Selling Expenses," but accurately as
"Bribes." And, they should be disclosed. Obviously, correct recording and disclosure is often less than feasible, particularly in the
country in which the bribe is paid; so the proposals were expected
to prevent the payments.

The proposals appealed to Congress, and late in 1977 it passed
PL 95-213, "The Foreign Corrupt Practices Act of 1977." Early
drafts of the Act included extremely restrictive language concerning internal controls and accounting systems and the recording of
illegal payments. After intensive lobbying by the AICPA, the bill
was amended to reflect the conventional language the accounting
profession uses to define internal controls. The Act requires companies subject to the Securities Acts to:

A. make and keep books, records, and accounts, which, in reasonable
   detail, accurately and fairly reflect the transactions and dispositions
   of the assets of the issuer; and

B. devise and maintain a system of internal accounting controls sufficient to provide reasonable assurances that—
   (i)   transactions are executed in accordance with management's general or specific authorization;
   (ii) transactions are recorded as necessary (I) to permit preparation of financial statements in conformity with generally accepted accounting principles or any other criteria applicable to such statements, and (II) to maintain accountability for assets;
   (iii) access to assets is permitted only in accordance with management's general or specific authorization; and
   (iv) the recorded accountability for assets is compared with the existing assets at reasonable intervals and appropriate action is taken with respect to any differences.

Having established the internal control and accounting record requirements for public companies, the Act then prohibits shareholders, officers, and employees of both publicly-held and private corporations from making or authorizing payments to foreign officials, political parties, or third parties for the purpose of:

A. Influencing any act or decision of such foreign official in his official capacity, including a decision to fail to perform his official functions; or
B. inducing such foreign official to use his influence with a foreign government or instrumentality thereof to affect or influence any act or decision of such government or instrumentality, in order to assist such issuer (or private concern) in obtaining or retaining business for or with, or directing business to any person. . . .

(The provisions affecting private corporations are a part of the U.S. Code, while those affecting companies whose shares are publicly traded are part of the Securities Exchange Act of 1934.)

This is a unique, challenging, and possibly ominous extension of the responsibilities of accountants and the internal accounting control system to what is clearly governance of the actions of the corporation. The Act not only forbids actions which may not be illegal in other countries, but it also requires the design of a corporate control system to prevent the actions.

I believe that this is the first example of legislation with these characteristics: forbidding a series of actions of the corporations and placing responsibility on the accounting and control systems for their prevention. Thus, the accountants are made direct agents in the control mechanism.

However, a familiar problem now returns. As discussed above, there are distinct limitations on the abilities of accountants and accounting control systems. Controls are not effective against managers, and modest amounts or transactions through third parties can easily be concealed. While not explicit in the law, it would appear that the corporate auditors will be required to consider the functioning of this element of internal controls in their usual examinations. This will require audit procedures which, once again, may be outside of the usual competence of auditors.

Accountants and Auditors

The titles of accountant and auditor have deliberately been used interchangeably in this chapter. The distinction on a personal basis is meaningless. Auditors are accountants by profession and training. As auditors they remain accountants, but in the function of testing and commenting on the work of other accountants.

On a functional basis, the distinction may have more utility. The accountant is generally considered to work for the corporation; the independent auditor checks the work of the accountant. In discussions of financial reporting, particularly in the context of public disclosure and performance measurement, the distinction is valid and important. The corporate accountant may have a vested interest in biased measurements, while the outside auditor is expected to detect and correct any material evidence of such bias.

However, this chapter deals with accounting as a mechanism for the governance of the corporation. Attempts are being made to give the independent auditor either a separate role in governance or a cooperative one with the board of directors and audit committees. As a practical matter, however, the economics and logistics of a separate role for the independent auditor are dubious. The illegal payments or activities contemplated usually involve amounts which are insignificant compared to the amounts which are the subject of the normal audit. Employing independent auditors to search for such items on a regular basis would involve volumes of manpower which are probably not available, especially internationally, and prohibitive costs. The main burden of the work would undoubtedly fall on the corporate accountants and internal auditors, possibly advised by the independent auditors. A sharp distinction between corporate accountant and independent auditor in the area of corporate conduct will be· difficult to achieve.

The earlier part of this chapter was concerned with the development of accounting principles and the new efforts to utilize them as part of the mechanism for governance of the corporation. In the past, professional accountants—who are mainly auditors—dealt with the SEC as pronouncements were developed. However, with the establishment of the Financial Accounting Standards Board, separate from the AICPA, the link to the accounting profession was sharply weakened. Corporate accountants have gradually gained an increasing role in the operations of the SEC. At this writing the chairman of the board of trustees of the FASB is a corporate financial executive and corporate responses have dominated the comment letters and testimony given to the FASB on recent pronouncements. Increasingly, the private sector responsibility for the development of accounting principles and practices appears to be shared by an indistinguishable group of corporate and public accountants. The critical issue remains involved with the use of accounting and all accountants in corporate governance.

The Major Issues

This chapter has attempted to develop the contention that the principle issue of accounting in corporate governance relates to the use of accounting as a control device. If the idea of accounting as a control over behavior is accepted, then control of accounting itself becomes a significant issue.

Accounting principles have been developed, promulgated, and ultimately enforced for several decades under a partnership arrangement between the public accounting profession and the Securities and Exchange Commission. That relationship has recently been threatened by Congressional proposals and by private sector groups. The future of the relationship may be sharply affected by the outcome of the debate over the oil and gas company accounting, with the possible result being far stronger government control of accounting and financial reporting.

The SEC, Congress, and the public have recently shown great interest in the conduct of the corporation, particularly in the area of illegal and questionable payments. The initial investigations and the SEC voluntary program led to passage of the Foreign Corrupt Practices Act of 1977. This legislation makes U.S. corporate executives legally responsible for a wide range of foreign payments and actions and requires the establishment of internal accounting control systems designed to prevent such payments. The corporate accounting system is being used as a device for enforcing American concepts of corporate morality on a world-wide basis. Managements will be faced not only with coping with specific accounting demands, but with the impacts on their competitive position of being forbidden to undertake selling activities which are permitted to their principal foreign competitors.

SOME POSSIBLE SOLUTIONS: THE REPORT
OF THE COMMISSION ON AUDITORS' RESPONSIBILITIES

Professors, such as this writer, frequently assert that their task is completed if they have produced a detailed exposition and analysis of the problems. Solutions are left to others.

Unfortunately, I cannot use my academic background as an excuse for failing to suggest some answers to the problems I have described. From 1974 to 1978 I eschewed academe and instead directed the day-to-day operations of a "blue-ribbon" commission established to study what auditors should do.

The Commission on Auditors' Responsibilities was established by the AICPA in October 1974. The chairman was Manuel Cohen, former chairman of the Securities and Exchange Commission. The other six members were drawn from public accounting, financial analysis, banking, and, in my case, academe. The Commission's final report includes more than sixty recommendations for improvement, many of which will impact the areas which were described earlier in this chapter.

DISSATISFACTION WITH ACCOUNTING AND THE
PREFERABILITY ISSUE

In the first section of this chapter, I suggested that the present dissatisfaction with the performance of accountants and auditors, as expressed by many critics including several Congressional committees, could lead to greater government control over accounting and auditing. The situation has arisen principally because of widespread dissatisfaction with the performance of accountants and auditors during the rapidly changing business environment of the 1960s.

Our Commission addressed this issue and concluded that the performance of accountants and auditors was indeed lacking during this period and that the substantial investor dissatisfaction was warranted. It appears that the problem sprung from two failures on the part of the accounting profession. First, the authoritative bodies charged with promulgating accounting principles and practices failed to keep pace with the rapidly changing business environment. Many companies in new industries for which specific accounting pronouncements did not exist were free to establish their own often innovative and privately advantageous systems of accounting. This failure was well known to the accounting profession and ultimately resulted in the dismissal of the AICPA's Accounting Principles Board and the transfer of its functions to the new, independent body, the Financial Accounting Standards Board.

The failure to promulgate new accounting principles might have been alleviated had some independent auditors acted in a more professional manner. The second failure was that auditors often interpreted the lack of authoritative accounting pronouncements to mean that the companies in the new industries were, indeed, free to select their own accounting practices, creative though they may be. Too many auditors believed that so long as the company selected accounting principles and practices which were minimally acceptable, no further guidance was required from the auditor.

The Commission on Auditors' Responsibilities emphatically disagreed with this belief and made what I believe, in the long run, will be its most important recommendation. The Commission recommended that generally accepted auditing standards should include a requirement that the independent auditor determine that his client has selected the accounting principles and practices which are "preferable" in the circumstances, whenever alternatives exist and a rational choice can be made among them. The Commission believes that had this requirement been articulated during the 1960s, many of the problems and the resulting dissatisfaction with auditors would not have occurred.

There is considerable opposition to this proposal on the part of some auditors and many corporate financial executives. Indeed, it is probably the most controversial one made by the Commission. Nevertheless, on the assumption that the American business community will continue to evolve rapidly and that the Financial Accounting Standards Board will never be completely current with the latest changes in business, the independent auditors must be required to exercise their individual, professional judgment on a continuing basis.

A PRIVATE SECTOR APPROACH TO ILLEGAL AND
QUESTIONABLE PAYMENTS

An earlier section of this chapter discussed the continuing controversy over illegal acts and payments made by the corporations. It has been strongly suggested that independent auditors should accept significant responsibility for the detection and prevention of such acts.

On the other hand, independent auditors, conscious of their relative inability to find such acts, have attempted to eschew responsibility. The Commission believed that in the present environment, auditors could not avoid responsibility in this area, nor, however, should they suddenly be required to assume responsibilities which are incommensurate both with their abilities and training.

To cope with these dual problems, the Commission proposed that corporations should first be required to develop and articulate detailed statements of policy which say precisely which acts are forbidden to their employees. Such statements should give careful consideration to the usual business practices in the company's industry. The statements should be published or otherwise disseminated to both employees and shareholders.

We believe that the dissemination of the policy statements on illegal and questionable acts to shareholders is necessary in order to provide broad, informed concurrence with the corporate policies in an admittedly difficult area. If the published policies are unsatisfactory to shareholders, they will obviously have to be revised until a consensus on appropriate conduct is reached.

Thereafter, top management of the corporation, in consultation with its independent auditors, would be expected to make whatever practicable changes are required in the corporate system of internal accounting control in order to maximize conformity with the stated policies and to minimize the possibility of avoidance without detection. In many cases it will be necessary to restrict some of the authority of top management to give sole approval to disbursements and other transactions and to expand the activities of internal auditors.

If these steps are taken, it would then be feasible for independent auditors to provide a reasonable degree of assurance that management and the other corporate employees are obeying the stated policies on illegal and questionable activities. Providing such assurance will require auditors to modify and extend some of their present audit procedures, but we believe that these changes will be accomplished at reasonable costs. The Commission also believes in the importance of taking action on a voluntary basis, before the imposition of additional government controls over corporate conduct.

REPORTING ON INTERNAL ACCOUNTING CONTROLS

Closely related to the Commission's recommendations in the area of illegal and questionable acts is a recommendation that independent auditors report publicly on the functioning of the corporate system of internal accounting control. This recommendation was based both on the receipt by the Commission of indications from many users of financial information that they desired such assurances and on the Commission's belief that the importance of internal accounting control has grown to the point where directors, investors, and creditors ought to receive assurances about the functioning of the system.

Another aspect of the Report of the Commission is to provide users of financial information with a clearer conception of the division of duties between management and auditors. The financial statements are representations by management; the auditor comments on the validity of those representations. The financial statements contained in the usual annual report include an opinion only from the independent auditors. There is no indication that the statements are, in fact, the representations of the management of the corporation. It is no wonder that a survey conducted by the Commission indicated that a majority of investors believed that financial statements are prepared by the auditors. In order to provide a vehicle for better understanding on the part of the users of financial statements and to fulfill many of the recommendations of the Commission, we proposed that management issue a report with the financial statements. Management should state that it prepared the financial statements in accord with generally accepted accounting principles and that it believed that the principles were appropriately applied in the circumstances. Several companies, including General Motors, issued such a management report with their 1977 annual reports. A copy of the Commission's proposed management report is reproduced at the end of this chapter.

The Commission also suggested that the management report on the financial statements would be the appropriate vehicle for representations regarding the system of internal control and the efficacy of the policies and control systems related to illegal and questionable acts.

The initial representation as to the state of the corporation's system of internal accounting control would therefore appear in the management report. The auditor's opinion would include a reference to that representation and an evaluation of its accuracy. In the event, however, that management wishes not to make a representation regarding its system of internal accounting control, the Commission recommended that auditors be required to report, in their opinion, material uncorrected deficiencies in internal controls.

RESPONSIBILITIES FOR CORPORATE DIRECTORS

The Commission on Auditors' Responsibilities considered the growing importance of audit committees of boards of directors and, in general, endorsed the trend. The members of the Commission believed, however, that the variety and the circumstances of corporations are such that the responsibilities frequently attributed to audit committees should be considered to be the responsibilities of the board as a whole, delegated, if appropriate, to a particular committee.

A survey conducted for the Commission also resulted in a recommendation that the board of directors should take an active and direct role in negotiating the scope of the audit and the fee with the independent auditors. The study consisted of an examination of the work habits and professional attitudes of a large sample of independent auditors. Much to the Commission's dismay, some of the survey results indicated consistent unprofessional conduct by some independent auditors. The unprofessional conduct appeared to stem from two major causes. In many cases, corporate management, eager to make early issuance of annual reports and registration statements, appeared to place excessive time pressures on the auditors. The other significant factor appeared to be the time pressures originating within the auditing firm caused principally by excessive concern with the total cost of the audit which, in turn, appeared to be caused by excessive competition among auditing firms.

It is obviously difficult, in the free market of the United States, to propose that competition be limited. However, the Commission believes that boards of directors have a better perspective on the trade-offs between audit quality and fees than the corporate managers who frequently negotiate with the independent auditors.

Conclusion: The Future

I am not so naive as to believe that all of the recommendations of the Commission on Auditors' Responsibilities will be instituted, although it is gratifying to note that several have already been adopted and many others are in process of adoption. Even if all of our suggestions were taken, all criticism and all attempts at increasing control over accounting would not be eliminated. Such attempts will be frustrated only by continued conscientious efforts on the part of corporate directors and managers, authoritative accounting bodies, and independent auditors to continually improve the financial reporting environment.

Report by Management *

Financial Statements

We prepared the accompanying consolidated balance sheet of XYZ Company as of December 31, 1976, and the related statements of consolidated income and changes in consolidated financial position for the year then ended, including the notes [or, (the named statements) have been prepared on our behalf by our independent auditor from the company's records and other relevant sources.]. The statements have been prepared in conformity with generally accepted accounting principles appropriate in the circumstances, and necessarily include some amounts that are based on our best estimates and judgments. The financial information in the remainder of this annual report [or other document] is consistent with that in the financial statements.

Internal Accounting Controls

The company maintains an accounting system and related controls to provide reasonable assurance that assets are safeguarded against loss from unauthorized use or disposition and that financial records are reliable for preparing financial statements and maintaining accountability for assets. There are inherent limitations that should be recognized in considering the potential effectiveness of any system of internal accounting control. The concept of reasonable assurance is based on the

* Illustration of Report by Management (as proposed by the Cohen Commission Report)

recognition that the cost of a system of internal control should not exceed the benefits derived and that the evaluation of those factors requires estimates and judgments by management. The company's system provides such reasonable assurance. We have corrected all material weaknesses of the accounting and control systems identified by our independent auditors, Test Check & Co., Certified Public Accountants [or, We are in the process of correcting all material weaknesses . . .] [or, We have corrected some of the material weaknesses but have not corrected others because. . . .].

Other Matters

The functioning of the accounting system and related controls is under the general oversight of the board of directors [or the audit committee of the board of directors]. The members of the audit committee are associated with the company only through being directors. The accounting system and related controls are reviewed by an extensive program of internal audits and by the company's independent auditors. The audit committee [or the board of directors] meets regularly with the internal auditors and the independent auditors and reviews and approves their fee arrangements, the scope and timing of their audits, and their findings.

We believe that the company's position in regard to litigation, claims and assessments is appropriately accounted for or disclosed in the financial statements. In this connection we have consulted with our legal counsel concerned with such matters and they concur with the presentation of the position.

The company has prepared and distributed to its employees a statement of its policies prohibiting certain activities deemed illegal, unethical, or against the best interests of the company. (The statement was included in the 197X annual report of the company; copies are available on request.) In consultation with our independent auditors we have developed and instituted additional internal controls and internal audit procedures designed to prevent or detect violations of those policies. We believe that the policies and procedures provide reasonable assurance that our operations are conducted in conformity with the law and with a high standard of business conduct.

[If applicable, During the past year our independent auditors provided the company with certain non-audit services. They advised us in the preparation of [or, if applicable, They prepared] the company's income tax return; they assisted in the design and installation of a new inventory control system; and they performed the actuarial computations in connection with the company's pension plan.]

[If applicable, The board of directors of the company in March, 1976 engaged Super, Sede & Co., Certified Public Accountants, as our independent auditors to replace Test Check & Co., following disagreements on [accounting principles, disclosures, or the scope of the examination]. Test Check & Co. agrees with that description of disagreements.]

I. M. True
Chief Financial Officer

John D. deButts

7

A Strategy
of Accountability

Introduction

Time was when most businesses in the United States counted
but three constituencies: customers, shareowners, and employees.
In recent years, to those three constituencies there has been added
a whole host of new ones: competitors, suppliers, neighbors, indeed
the public at large.

To my mind, so crucial is a balanced response to these multiple
constituencies that management dare not neglect any technique the
management sciences afford that might help.

In the final analysis, however, there is no substitute for the informed judgment of the chief executive officer who is ready to seek
out and enter those arenas where the interests of constituencies
converge and sometimes clash.

JOHN D. DEBUTTS *is Chairman of the Board and chief executive officer of
the American Telephone and Telegraph Company and Chairman of The
Business Council. A trustee of several philanthropic and civic organizations, he has received numerous achievement and leadership awards and
honorary degrees for his work in public affairs.*

I. The Proliferation of Corporate Constituencies

A HISTORICAL PERSPECTIVE

There was a time in this country when the entire industrial sector of many communities consisted of the separately and singly held property and talents of individuals. Some readers may still retain a childhood memory of a local independent cabinetmaker, tinker, wheelwright, cooper, or the like. Precious few of these entrepreneurs survive today. In their heyday they not only performed all their own work, but usually supplied their own raw materials and tools as well. They had a single constituency—their customers.

Those who succeeded—that is, those who survived the technological and economic caprices of the marketplace—eventually found need for assistants, and hence acquired, frequently from within their own family, a second constituency—employees. Fair treatment of these employees in terms of wages and working conditions became an additional concern of the craftsman.

Further growth of the business could lead to the need for outside financing to support expansion. As it did so, the two functions of "managing" and "owning" began to separate, and those "running the business"—now no longer, as a rule, practicing craftsmen—found themselves involved with, and accountable to, a third constituency —investors, the equivalent of today's shareholders and bondholders.

I do not wish to imply that most, or even many, of today's large corporations actually experienced an early development similar to that described in this simple illustration. Individual company histories are, in most cases, far more complex. But the illustration does serve to show how the growth of even the most modest enterprise—the efforts of a single individual—can lead naturally to the acquisition of multiple constituent groups.

THE THREE-LEGGED STOOL

I can recall the time when it was common to use the analogy of a three-legged stool to make the point that management's role was, in fact, to seek and maintain a balance of interests among just three constituencies—customers, shareowners, and employees. I am told that in the 1950s, Thomas J. Watson, Sr., then chairman of the board of IBM, insisted upon systematically changing the order in which he mentioned those three constituencies in successive talks and speeches. That was his method of stressing their equality.

But times have changed and we seldom hear of three-legged stools anymore.

I have tried, unsuccessfully, to think of what would serve as a modern day replacement for our now outdated three-legged stool. The only image which recurs with uncomfortable persistence is not a piece of furniture at all. It's a porcupine—with the quills reversed.

For to the traditional constituencies of business have since been added a whole host of new constituencies encompassing the interest, general and specific, of the entire public and those who speak or profess to speak in its behalf: legislators, regulators, consumer advocates, environmentalists, activists of just about every kind and persuasion. In attempting to balance the diverse demands of such varied constituencies, all that today's managers can be certain of is that what best serves everybody will meet the perfect satisfaction of nobody. Nonetheless they try.

TECHNOPOLITICS

An often remarked aspect of our times is the degree to which government has come to play a role in business decisions hitherto private. Even for those of us in traditionally regulated industries, recent years have brought a vast expansion in the range of matters on which government has come to exercise an influential "say."

Not too many years ago, for example, most managers in the telephone industry thought that what the industry's technology made possible, the industry would in due course do. For most of the industry's history that perception was an accurate one. Recent history has taught us otherwise. More particularly, the Congressional debates over the ownership and operation of communication satellites in the early 1960s introduced us to the world of what our company's principal witness before Congress in those days called "technopolitics." We've been living in that world ever since. Today we in the industry know that there are a great many people besides ourselves who have a say in the way what we once called "our" business is run, people whose interests and views must somehow be accommodated in the decisions we make, in the decisions our regulators make. Indeed, in the face of continuing contentions over the aims of the nation's telecommunications policy and the way the telecommunications industry should be structured to fulfill those aims, we ourselves have said, "Let the public decide." We acknowledge that some of our most important strategic planning decisions depend on the resolution of issues which cannot be resolved entirely within the telecommunications industry. In short, we await the judgment of our constituents.

I would surmise that almost every major business in the country has had a like experience, and in all probability, more than once. Certainly the opportunity for interaction with government constituencies, as evidenced by their large number, would seem to support such a conjecture. For not only is every legislature, federal and state, in actuality a collection of multiple constituencies, each with its own specific concerns and interests, but so too are the executive branches, with dozens upon dozens of divisions and bureaus, each having its own particular responsibilities and authorities. Within the government also reside the independent regulatory agencies, whose growth in number and size seems to continue without limit. Recent additions at the federal level include the Equal Employment Opportunity Commission (1965), the Environmental Protection Agency (1970), the Consumer Products Safety Commission (1972), and the Nuclear Regulatory Commission (1975).

But it is not alone in the government arena that businesses confront a proliferation of new constituencies that business managers in earlier days might have thought would altogether overwhelm anyone's capacity to cope with them. The customer body of many businesses is also becoming progressively more and more diversified. In the telephone business, for example, it no longer makes sense to talk of a residence market and a business market, a simple market division we used for nearly a hundred years. Today, within each of these major divisions, there are many markets. Our business success depends on the degree to which we meet the distinctive requirements of each without compromise of all.

Businesses confront a like proliferation of new constituencies within their employee bodies and among the citizenry of the communities in which they operate. Separate and specific demands of various employee groups must be separately and specifically addressed, just as the distinctive requirements of the various customer markets. So too must be the public expectations of a company's presence in a city, town, or countryside, whether that presence takes the form of a power station, a manufacturing site, a business office, or a microwave antenna.

Nor are shareowners any longer a single constituency. Certainly account needs to be taken of the sometimes divergent interests of individual investors and institutional holders. But beyond that crude classification, management today is confronted with literally scores of miniconstituencies, many of them representing but a small fraction of the total shareowner body, but each feeling that it has a unique claim to the management's attention and a unique stake in the company's performance. In addition, consumerists, environmentalists, and a variety of citizens' action groups have chosen to seek representation as shareholder constituencies of many corporations.

COMPLEXITY COMPOUNDED

But the increased complexity of the corporate environment is not all manifested simply in the growing number of corporate constituencies. Two other factors, in particular, complicate the situation and greatly increase the difficulty of understanding or analyzing events and options for action in the corporate environment. First is the fact—perhaps too obvious to mention—that many of a corporation's constituencies are themselves constituencies of each other. Special interest groups (consumerists, environmentalists, etc.) and various government agencies provide an example.

A further complication is that membership in one constituency does not preclude membership in another. Thus, to the extent that separate constituent demands are in conflict, the interests and motives of an individual belonging to both of those constituencies will be less than obvious. Examples of individual membership in multiple constituencies abound. For the Bell System, the overwhelming majorities of the memberships of almost all its constituencies—government, suppliers, employees, shareholders, etc.—are also customers, and many of our employees are shareholders. Obviously then, there are a number of individuals who represent all three legs of the three-legged stool; some, doubtless, represent other constituencies as well.

For those who are attempting to balance multiple constituent interests, the added difficulties introduced by these two complications can be severe. First, largely because of the diversity of the overlapping memberships of many constituencies, it is frequently difficult to determine beforehand the strength of a particular constituency's response—or even whether that response will be positive or negative —to a given corporate decision (or action). Second, any complete analysis of a proposed corporate action obviously needs to include not only an understanding of the possible alternative responses of each constituency, but, in addition, the reactions of all other constituencies to those initial constituent responses. In essence, any significant corporate action can set in motion multiple chain reactions as the various corporate constituencies adjust and then readjust, first to the initial corporate action and subsequently to the various constituencies' reactions. Stated differently, corporate actions can upset interconnected equilibriums among the various constituencies in the corporate environment and cause multiple reverberations in the interactions among those constituencies before new equilibriums are established.

Understanding the likely secondary and tertiary consequences of various proposed alternative actions is not an easy job. Despite what I might wish, I cannot claim that we in the Bell System have become experts at such analyses. But we can certainly claim to be veterans of the experience as, over the last decade, we have time after time taken action in response to a demand of a particular constituency (typically the government) and found ourselves adjusting and then readjusting to the actions and reactions of other constituencies (typically our customers).

Making these adjustments wisely is the aim of strategic planning.

II. The Role of Strategic Planning

At the outset of our consideration of the role of strategic planning in the governance of corporations, let me make it plain that I know of no corporate strategic planning process—nor can I imagine one—so assured that it can remove the uncertainties and resolve the complexities that beset management in the face of proliferating constituencies.

But can strategic planning help? The answer to that question is most assuredly "yes." Moreover, I believe that helping management achieve a reasoned balance in its response to its varied constituencies is the most important function of the corporate strategic planning process.

What makes this task important, of course, is the prospect that whether the American people will continue to entrust to business those responsibilities that have in the past been business'—or, alternatively, will entrust them to other hands—will depend on the degree to which the public is ready to agree that business has fulfilled its accountabilities and thereby shown itself deserving of trust. Once again we hear raised a question formerly addressed to emperors and kings: quo warranto? (by what right do ye govern?) Only this time the question is being addressed to business. By what right do we decide? In reply, we in business can claim no right except what we can prove through performance. Only by matching our performance to society's diverse expectations can we confirm the legitimacy of corporate decision-making.

The task is not easy. The number and diversity of interest groups who have or think they have a stake in his business performance confronts today's manager with a degree of complexity beside which the complexities of our technology pale in comparison. And to help us cope with those new complexities we have no econometric models, no computer programs to quantify precisely our obligations to each of our newly emergent constituencies and to assign priorities among them. We have only our own perceptions. Organizing those perceptions is the first step in strategic planning.

THE PLANNING PROCESS

Strategic planning is the process by which a corporation seeks to match its unique competence and resources to external economic opportunities and threats—market demand; competitors' strengths and vulnerabilities; and forecasted economic, political, and social conditions.

Strategic planning decisions are those decisions which set corporate objectives, allocate resources to be used in reaching them, and establish policies which will govern that process. In short, strategic planning aims to match corporate capabilities with society's wants and needs.

These definitions, conventional as they are, remain as apt today as they were when corporate strategic planning first emerged as a distinguishable discipline a decade or more ago.

But while the words remain the same, their meaning, in practical terms, is radically different today from what it was even ten short years ago. For no longer can it be assumed that a corporation's competence and resources will be measured simply in terms of economics: technological and marketing competence, work force capabilities, financial resources, etc. And no longer are society's wants and needs, vis-à-vis business, measured strictly in terms of marketplace demand. Instead, the corporation is now viewed as having a wide variety of responsibilities transcending the marketplace. Some of those responsibilities are responsibilities to society at large. Whether a business has social responsibilities is, I know, a subject of widespread debate. But to my mind, it is a debate that continues long after the argument is over. Today I know of no leader of business who sees his function as limited to the pursuit of profit. I know of none who does not realize that the business that for profit's sake ignores the impacts of its actions on society is not likely to make a profit very long. In short, it has come to be widely recognized that to focus strategic planning activities on market opportunities alone is insufficient and may, in fact, be counterproductive.

NEW TOOLS

Corporate strategic planning is not new. Either deliberately or intuitively it has been practiced by the management of every serious private enterprise, large or small, from its beginning. However, the changing social, economic, and political environments; the increasing complexity of large-scale enterprise and society in general; and the growing availability of a wide variety of new sophisticated analytic techniques have all combined to alter drastically the "old way" of strategic planning. As a result, and as with so many other management functions, the planning process is far different today from what it was even a few years ago. In short, strategic planning has become—out of business necessity—a discipline.

In my own experience, the single most important new tool of planning—indeed management—is the computer. Analytic exercises of such scale and complexity as to have been unthinkable twenty years ago are now routinely performed on an almost daily basis. Coupled with the development and/or refinement of a variety of techniques (simulations, Delphi, trend impact analysis, etc.), computer outputs now provide corporate planning staffs—and ultimately corporate management—with an array of forecasts, projections, extrapolations, and interpolations that would have been astounding to corporate managers at the time I was beginning my career in the Bell System.

Sophisticated techniques, however, do not in themselves assure better decisions. We would deceive ourselves, it seems to me, if the sheer volume of data available to today's strategic planners and the apparent precision of their analyses led us to assume that we are thereby automatically provided with better answers. Obviously, objective analysis is a prerequisite to sound decision-making. But the day is not at hand—nor do I see it coming—when management decisions on the things that count most can rely entirely on objective analyses, however elaborate. Always they will involve risk and uncertainty. Always they will—for better or worse—reflect subjective judgments.

INTEGRATING STRATEGIC PLANNING

Because judgment is so large a factor in strategic planning, it seems to me a mistake to assign the function to a specialized elite insulated from the pressures and contradictions of everyday operating experience. Rather, strategic planning must be integrated with the on-going processes of management. Crucial is the personal commitment of the chief executive officer, a matter to which I shall return later. Beyond that, I count five basic ingredients necessary for strategic planning:

1. knowledge of constituent demands,
2. an understanding of environmental trends,
3. a method of integrating and analyzing that knowledge and understanding,
4. effective internal communications, and
5. individual accountability of managers.

Some brief comments on how each of these factors fits into the strategic planning process follow.

Constituent Demands—Obviously, contending with constituent demands requires an understanding, as accurate as possible, of what each significant constituency is currently demanding of the corporation. That understanding is necessary not to enable a corporation to comply more specifically with each and every demand—far from it. Clearly, compliance with demands that are in conflict is impossible. Rather, I simply suggest that only with a thorough understanding of all constituent interests can an effective balance of those interests be maintained.

Nor should it be assumed because I counsel understanding of constituency demands that in every instance I counsel accommodation. Some constituency demands are wrongheaded. Some are impossible—or too costly—to meet. Some would involve a sacrifice of principle.

But these demands, too, require understanding. For if they are not met, they must nonetheless be answered.

Environmental Trends—Concurrent with, and not unrelated to, the proliferation of corporate constituencies over the last fifteen years has been a series of profound changes in the environment within which business operates. These changes have included enormous technological advances (space travel, the computer, and now microprocessors), important demographic shifts (the movement from cities to suburbia, the migration to the "sun belt," etc.), social upheavals (minority rights, women's liberation, "gray power"), severe economic swings (booms, recessions, and recoveries), and dramatic political turns, domestic and international.

Such changes plainly can alter, in a fundamental way, not only the makeup and views of various constituencies, but also the ability of a corporation to respond to constituent demands. Effective corporate strategic planning clearly must take into account such environmental changes. Early recognition and understanding of developing trends provide a basis for making assessments of possible future changes. These assessments in turn provide the means by which future demands on the corporation can be anticipated.

Integration and Analysis—Whether the information regarding constituent demands and environmental trends is collected and cataloged in some highly structured formal system, or whether it is simply acquired in day to day activities of the corporate staff and officers and passed along in conversation, I believe that an integrated analysis of those two factors must, of necessity, constitute a major input in the development of today's corporate strategic plans.

I suspect the staffs of U.S. corporations began to integrate these elements into their planning processes many years ago. Most, I suspect, do so informally, relying on a broad array of information collecting devices, from public opinion and attitude surveys to the reports of officers in informal conversations at business luncheons.

Establishing the relevance of specific societal trends to the interests of specific businesses is one of the more difficult tasks in incorporating social goals and public preferences in strategic planning. Experts in public issues frequently cannot make a useful translation of their knowledge to a specific business because they simply do not know enough about that business. Business managers, on the other hand, frequently tend to underestimate the power and influence of prevailing social trends on their operations. There is no easy formula by which a manager can deal with this aspect of planning. Awareness of the problem, however, can emphasize the need for recognizing the rare individual, having sufficient currency in both fields, who has the knack of establishing good linkage between them.

Effective Internal Communications—Often overlooked but crucial to effective strategic planning is the timely communication of corporate policies and positions within the corporation. Without clear understanding of corporate policies, at the appropriate time, on the part of all employees, it is apparent that corporate behavior—in effect, the actions of those employees—cannot accurately reflect corporate strategic planning decisions. Too many instances in my own career, on both the giving and receiving end of that dialogue, have served to confirm my view that this task is much more difficult —and more crucial—than it is generally assumed to be. Policy, unless it is communicated, isn't policy at all.

At AT&T we have recently undertaken to clarify explicitly, for both our shareholders and our employees, basic company policies regarding several important areas of our business. We began with a comprehensive statement of those policies, read and critiqued by principal members of top management. This statement was reviewed by our board of directors and published as part of our annual report. Each employee, nearly one million in total, received a copy.

Individual Accountability—Perhaps the single most important factor in determining whether business can win the public's trust is the quality of the accountability each individual manager exercises on a day-to-day basis. As I suggested above, ensuring an understanding of corporate policies on the part of all managers and keeping them current regarding strategic planning decisions is not an easy task. But the importance of that activity cannot be overemphasized. How well business will be understood depends, first of all, on how well business' own managers understand.

III. The Role of the Chief Executive Officer

By their very nature, strategic decisions on matters of real consequence must be made in the absence of sufficient information to assure that they are right. In short, no matter how authoritative the experts, how explicit the assumptions, or how voluminous the supporting data, speculation and analysis end before a clear conclusion emerges.

When all of the experts have departed, it is the chief executive officer, relying on personal knowledge and experience, who must assess the situation, weigh the alternatives, and make the decision. Although a variety of analytic assessments may—to a greater or lesser degree—be available for information and guidance, the final act of decision-making will always be a highly subjective one—a judgment call.

How well CEOs are equipped, personally, to make the "right" decisions depends, to a large extent, on how directly and personally involved they have been in the various interactions—confrontation sometimes—which continually take place between a corporation and its constituencies. In my own view, there is no substitute for personal experience of those interactions, experience that cannot be gained in the splendid isolation of the executive suite. In my view, the chief executive officer serves his company best—and perhaps his own composure least—who is ready to seek out those arenas where interests converge and sometimes clash and to place himself—deliberately and squarely—in their midst.

To my mind, the chief executive officer who does not do so neglects what may be the first responsibility of his job, that of spokesmanship.

SPOKESMANSHIP

By spokesmanship I mean something more than oratorical skill or a talent for apt rejoinder to queries from the press. On the contrary, the first requirement of effective spokesmanship is effective listening. As I have said elsewhere, spokesmanship requires, first of all, an acute sensitivity to the concerns of other people—the ability to stand in the other fellow's shoes, so to speak. It calls for discernment of what will work from what won't, what will pay from what won't, and, most important of all, what is right from what is wrong. It calls for the courage to be candid, to say what needs to be said in the face of the certain knowledge that some people might not want to hear it. And, finally, it calls for a kind of persuasiveness that derives—more than it does from eloquence—from the power of honest conviction.

The Annual Meeting—Perhaps in no other forum does the CEO have a greater opportunity to exercise spokesmanship than at his company's annual meeting. If evidence were needed of the proliferation of corporate constituencies, today's annual meetings provide it. No longer do agendas of these assemblies deal solely with the traditional (largely economic) concerns of faithful shareowners who dutifully listen to management's accounting of its performance and as dutifully vote for such resolutions as management endorses and against those it opposes. Instead, the CEO chairing such a meeting today must be prepared to cope with challenges that range across the entire spectrum of public concerns—many of them matters which twenty years ago might have been ruled "out of order" on grounds of irrelevance to the business at hand.

The Board of Directors—Preparing for such encounters—indeed to prepare himself for all his relationships with his business' diverse constituencies—the CEO has available in a properly constituted board of directors a most useful resource from which to draw counsel on how best to meet his company's public obligations. More and more such obligations extend beyond the immediate and readily identifiable interests of shareowners, customers, and employees. In attempting to fulfill those obligations, assuring a balanced response to society's interests and concerns, outside directors can bring valuable perspectives and insights to board discussions.

Some have proposed that boards of directors be reconstituted on a constituency basis to reflect the major elements of our society—minorities, labor unions, consumers, etc. It is not to deny that currently some corporate boards are drawn from too narrow a base that I say at the same time that constituency representation will not work in the governance of a corporation. It flies in the face of the fact that directors are by law—and should be in fact—responsible to the entire body of shareowners, not to this or that faction among them. More fundamentally it will not work because in the governance of corporations one person's opinion is not as good as another's. To politicize the process would supplant competence with compromise, timely decision with intolerable delay, and genuine conviction with political maneuver.

Recent years have seen a variety of changes in composition and operation of the boards of directors of many corporations. A number of these changes have been aimed specifically at equipping the board to achieve a balanced response to society's interests and concerns. Among such changes, and one I commend from personal experience, is the growing use of Public Policy Committees of the board. Such committees provide a focus for board discussion of the company's obligations in the realm of social policy, and they can vastly enlarge the context within which corporate decisions are made and actions taken.

Conclusion

Always in a dynamic society there are mismatches between traditional institutional arrangements and current realities. Currently there is a mismatch between traditional corporate forms and processes and the demands of the corporation's new constituencies. Some argue that this mismatch is so great that only fundamental restructuring of the rules of corporate governance will suffice to close it. I do not agree.

While it would be naive to suggest that all corporations are responding to changed circumstances at a sufficient pace, it is, I believe, equally misguided to assert that a rational accommodation cannot be made. Indeed, it is being made. What is more, it is being made at business' own initiative and not as a consequence of compulsion. What I hope I have conveyed here is a sense of the urgency of a continuation of those initiatives and the importance in this regard of an active board of directors, an involved chief executive, and a strategic planning process that explicitly takes account of constituency demands and social goals.

Melvin Anshen

8

Governance Issues
within the
Corporate Management Structure

The principal current issues of corporate governance are not limited to changes in relationships between corporations and governmental institutions and between corporations and various external constituencies and "publics." Nor are changes within the corporate organization limited to the board of directors and the chief executive officer.

Corporate governance issues external to and within the corporation are a seamless web. Adaptation to change in the corporation's external relationships must be accompanied by parallel adaptation within the corporation. The ultimate goal of revisions in governance from outside is change in corporate behavior. Issues of policy and practice must therefore be dealt with inside the corporate management structure below the level of the board and the chief executive officer. These issues involve both the systems through which objectives, policies, and strategies are formulated and implemented and patterns of management performance. They concern the beliefs,

MELVIN ANSHEN *is Paul Garrett Professor of Public Policy and Business Responsibility at Columbia University. He is a director or consultant to several major corporations. Professor Anshen has written a number of major works on business problems, including* Managing the Socially Responsible Corporation.

attitudes, and motivations of all levels of the administrative hierarchy. This extends from the senior management group that participates with directors and chief executive officers in determining fundamental policies down to the middle and junior managers without whose understanding and commitment the execution of policies will falter and even fail.

There is an additional reason for considering governance issues within the management structure. The same societal forces that have stimulated criticism of the external aspects of corporate behavior have also encouraged reassessment of the experiences of individuals within business organizations. Corporations not only affect the economic and social condition of society; they are themselves social organisms within which a substantial share of the population receives much of their life experience—directly for those employed, indirectly for their families. What happens to individuals within corporations is as legitimate an object for critical review as is the network of relationships between the corporation and its external environment.

The Role of Top Management

Top corporate management—specifically the board of directors, the chief executive officer, and his immediate associates—is solely responsible for the decision to commit an organization with respect to social and economic performance. This responsibility is grounded in the fact that such a decision will shape the long-term character of a business and its operating results. It will influence the design and enter the content of strategic planning. It will affect the allocation of resources. It will alter middle management assignments together with the standards and procedures used in evaluating their performance. It will change personnel policies and practices. In sum, it will determine both the real ethos of a company and the perception of that ethos by employees at all levels and by external publics.

Any top level commitment, however, requires a fully-developed plan for its execution. Where that plan involves, as do changes in the balance of economic and social goals, an innovation in business philosophy that many subordinates will view as breaking with traditional management doctrine, the chief executive officer and his senior associates bear a special responsibility. They must articulate principle and supply example. They must instruct, persuade, and counsel. They must think through and engineer adaptations in internal governance structure, motivation, and operating systems that will facilitate the transition. By statement and action they must overcome skepticism, inertia, even opposition grounded in perceived self-interest or in different views of what is best for the company.

Broad pronouncements without follow-through are likely to expose the chief executive officer to charges of hypocrisy or cosmetic public relations. If many major corporations are perceived by employees and the public as vulnerable to such criticism, the general decline of confidence in the business system and the parallel deterioration in the credibility of business leaders, both so marked in recent years, will be reinforced to a degree that will make restoration of trust extremely difficult.

INTEGRATION OF SOCIAL AND ECONOMIC PERFORMANCE

The case for an integrated approach to all aspects of a company's social and economic performance is underscored by observed deficiencies of fragmented approaches. Some firms, for example, have singled out employment of minorities as a special object of attention and have created the position of "manager of minority relations" or "urban affairs officer," usually under the administrative jurisdiction of a staff vice president with responsibility for personnel relations or public and governmental relations. Some companies have focused on the cultivation of minority-owned suppliers and have designated a staff position with a mission to encourage, monitor, and assist procurement from such suppliers. In some organizations the primary interest has been to reduce environmental pollution or upgrade hygiene and safety for workers, and staffing has reflected this emphasis. In some, the focal issue has been improving consumer relations, again with designation of a special officer to define relevant policies and programs.

Such fragmented efforts exhibit common deficiencies on both conceptual and operating levels. On the conceptual level, a fragmented approach encourages senior managers to regard each specific program as a self-sufficient response to a special societal requirement. This reduces the likelihood that top managers will recognize and evaluate the emergence of a new environment for business in the form of a comprehensive and interrelated set of performance expectations. If they do not see things as a whole, they cannot orient and educate middle managers appropriately. The result is a continual lag in grasping the full meaning of emerging governance conditions for the business system.

This conceptual deficiency has serious operating implications. It discourages introducing social performance considerations into the strategic planning process. It gets in the way of any effort to anticipate the effects of evolving public attitudes. It fails to illuminate the necessity for revising the duties of middle managers and for adapting performance evaluation systems to the enlarged operating assignments. It inhibits efforts to develop meaningful cost-benefit analyses. Above all, it instills throughout the organization a sense of defensive and grudging accommodation to unreasonable and undesirable restrictions, a syndrome of resisting change. As a result, management loses its ability to execute its primary mission of maximizing economic performance.

EFFECTS ON MANAGEMENT ATTITUDES AND PERFORMANCE

Fragmentation also damages organization structure and behavior. Each special program is usually assigned to a discrete staff function within an established administrative activity group. Staff specialists have the task of developing policies, standards, and procedures and then working through indirect lines of persuasion to get operating managers to accept and implement the program.

Conflicts already exist between traditional line economic performance objectives and new social performance objectives. Since line managers associate the first with performance evaluation and the reward/penalty system, judgments about relative priorities tend to subordinate the new social programs to what line managers perceive as primary goals. This confusion is compounded by competition among staff officers for line managers' attention to different social programs. Requests for guidance and adjudication that move up the organizational hierarchy are received by senior line officers who themselves have no explicit social performance responsibilities but do have economic performance responsibilities. The resulting decision problems are rendered even more complex when, as is usually the case, line managers are under pressure to accomplish short-term results. Most social programs have visible short-run costs and, by traditional measures, ill-defined long-run payoffs.

If there is no clearly articulated commitment by the chief executive officer to specific performance objectives, no direct assignment of responsibility to his senior line associates to accomplish the objectives, and no guidance on priorities applicable in conflict situations, there will be skepticism about all aspects of social performance. Managers disposed to hostility toward what they see as subversion of corporate purpose or, even worse, a general attack on the integrity of the private enterprise system, are subjected to neither persuasion nor restraint. As critics, they can point out how hiring and promoting blacks and women raises costs and disturbs the morale and security of existing employees; how investing in pollution control yields no productive output and diverts money from profitable plant modernization and expansion; how modification of marketing practices to satisfy the complaints of consumer activists threatens competitive market positions and shrinks operating margins. Such managers will view staff-supported social policies and programs as peripheral matters, secondary to the "real work" of the business, at best worth only minor attention in the context of mainstream operations.

In effect on long-run corporate performance, the greatest danger of the piecemeal approach is the way it limits imaginative analysis of the full array of available strategic options. By focusing on one issue at a time, it encourages managers to think defensively and to ignore opportunities for taking initiatives. It fails to draw management attention to emerging situations in which the individual firm or the business community can recommend constructive proposals which would serve the public interest without creating unwieldy administrative bureaucracies or regulatory systems that are open invitations to inefficiency or corruption.

REQUIREMENTS FOR EFFECTIVE MANAGEMENT OF SOCIAL
AND ECONOMIC PERFORMANCE

The first requirement for effective management of corporate social performance is therefore a clear signal by the chief executive officer of personal responsibility for the decision to coordinate social and economic objectives in managing the business. This commitment must be demonstrated to all managers by precept and example. Only then can the corporate leader persuade skeptics and opponents and influence established patterns of thought and behavior. Anything less is likely to be appraised as "high-level public relations" in the pejorative sense of that abused term.

One of the most effective ways for the chief executive officer (CEO) to demonstrate the integrity of his commitment would be to take the lead in redesigning the composition, organization, and agenda of the board of directors. Important reinforcing evidence would be adaptation of the strategic planning process to incorporate social projections and the issuance of planning guidelines that include social performance considerations. Very few skeptics would remain in the management group if, in addition, the CEO delineated the revision of written descriptions of senior and middle managers' duties and responsibilities to include social performance standards in terms appropriate for each position and further provided for evaluation of managers' performance against these standards.

Administrative responsibility for social performance should not be delegated to a senior officer reporting to the CEO. A company's economic performance is always viewed as every manager's responsibility within the blueprint of a comprehensive planning and operating scheme. A company's social performance must rest on an equally broad base.

A second requirement is for the chief executive officer and his principal management associates to define the meaning of social performance in the specific context of the company's production and marketing processes, the geographic scope of its operations, employment conditions and employees' attitudes and expectations, competitive conditions, obligations of its community, and customer relationships. The concepts involved in such a definition will be novel to many managers. What is called for, however, parallels the familiar standards of economic performance that are laid down by the leadership of any well-managed corporation. Guidelines for economic performance (such as rate of growth, level of profitability, percentage return on invested capital, and scope of business activity) are routinely accepted and applied by senior and middle managers. Yet only on the relatively rare occasions when substantial changes in technological or economic circumstances require revision of established standards do most managers see the complex considerations and debates involved in formulating those standards.

It will be more difficult to create for the first time comparable standards for social performance. Managers lack experience for thinking in social performance terms and need a language of description and measurement. These are substantial but not overwhelming challenges.

The chief executive's definition of social performance goals needs to be specific and coordinated with the company's economic goals. Many leaders are well ahead of their own middle managers in perceiving social trends and their implications for business governance. Unless the boss articulates new goals clearly, some managers will not grasp what he is talking about, why he is concerned with societal governance issues, how the new viewpoint will affect operations, or what the impact will be on the responsibilities and duties of individual managers.

The conversion of concept to practice can be accomplished most effectively by talking about specific aspects of business behavior, specific standards of performance, specific changes in managers' jobs, and specific procedures for evaluating managers' execution of their new responsibilities. The description of these specifics is likely to be most credible if the underlying considerations are perceived to be pragmatic, if the limits of feasible corporate action are clearly identified, if the commitment to play a constructive role in the social and political governance process is strongly asserted, and if managers are assured of top-level support in handling the operational difficulties and frictions they can realistically anticipate in the initial phases of change.

DEFINING SOCIAL PERFORMANCE CONCEPTS

The chief executive has the task of defining concepts of social performance in terms of a three-dimensional matrix. The first dimension is concerned with varieties of possible action. At one end of the continuum are actions that must be taken because they are mandated by law or regulation from which there clearly is no recourse or reason to seek recourse. Most fair employment actions, but probably only a small proportion of other social performance actions, will be generally appraised as unquestionably within this category.

At the other end of the continuum is a category of real or alleged social performance actions urged by ignorant or naive reformers, or by ideological opponents of the market system. These proposals require vigorous opposition by business leaders and business institutions. Their implementation would weaken the market system, cripple incentives to invest, or compel business to commit resources wastefully. Examples of issues in this category are price or margin controls in circumstances other than national security emergencies, pure air standards which can only be attained by halting energy expansion or curtailing economic activity and related employment, and expansion of social benefits in ways that destroy business and individual incentives or cause destructive rates of inflation.

Between these extremes are two areas that deserve more subtle analysis. Here are found most of the difficult problems of strategic choice. The first area includes possible actions that are supported by strong and growing social pressures, although not yet mandated by law or administrative order. The lesson of relevant history is unmistakable. In a political democracy, interest groups that express vigorous concern about specific perceived problems are likely to achieve the legislative resolution they propose unless other interest groups are equally vigorous both in their opposition and in steps to remove the underlying problems or propose more attractive alternative solutions.

From prohibition of alcoholic beverages to consumer protection bills, this scenario has played itself out repeatedly. Simple opposition to ill-considered and dangerous governance proposals designed to cope with problems that have captured substantial public attention is rarely a winning strategy. Even worse, continued opposition unaccompanied by alternative solutions communicates to a large share of the affected public the message that the interest of the business community is opposed to the broader public interest.

The nation's welfare and health care systems, however inefficient and ineffective, are what they are in good part because the business and professional communities opposed inept solutions to serious public needs advanced by other interests, but failed to design and fight for better alternatives. A widely-held public view is that business has been unreasonable and even irresponsible in its opposition to schemes for cleansing the air and water environment. The result has been, on one side, a dangerous failure to educate the public about the real costs of pushing environmental hygiene to its theoretical limits. On the other is an absence of any organized effort to study the relative effectiveness of the variety of different possible administrative approaches to cleansing the environment—such as performance specifications, user charges, or tax remission—each of which might be appropriate in a unique company or industry situation. The confusing and costly jungle of government actions to protect consumer interests is largely a product of the failure of business leadership to understand, articulate, and take action on behalf of the fundamental identity of business and consumer interests. The perceived passivity and indifference of business to consumers' complaints created opportunities for consumer activists to lobby successfully for legislative and regulatory solutions. The business community should never have appeared indifferent to these needs.

The other intermediate category involves areas where there may be special constraints on specific social performance actions. Such constraints, while not binding in all circumstances, may be substantial enough to justify careful exploration of the limits of maneuver and the economic or political costs of pushing the limits. Examples include union and employee relations in the context of nondiscriminatory promotion policies (particularly in implementing affirmative action programs designed to correct or compensate for prior discrimination), community relations in the context of environmental and plant hygiene policies, and trade relations in the context of consumer protection policies.

The second dimension of the matrix is concerned with distinctions among social performance actions that are feasible for one company; actions that, while not feasible for one company, are feasible for a group of companies (in a single industry or locality); and actions which require legislative or regulatory intervention, but to which business managers can contribute valuable technical or administrative guidance. In contrast to the first dimension, which lays out options with respect to what social performance actions may be feasible, this dimension identifies choices with respect to who can or should act.

Distinctions among single company, multicompany, and governmental social performance actions should be drawn in terms of practical considerations. A reasonable general decision rule would call for the individual corporation to act positively on opportunities for improving its responses to society's expectations for business behavior, subject to the constraint that no commitment should be made to policies or programs that would be likely to have a significant adverse effect on either profitability or competitive position. Where this constraint fits one company but not a group of companies in the same industry or geographic area, it is advantageous to seek voluntary coordinated action by a relevant group of companies. Where coordinated action is not feasible, because of either antitrust restrictions or the reluctance of potential collaborators, and where there is a strong probability of some kind of governmentally-mandated action, business leaders should try to help design the proposed legislative or regulatory action.

The general decision rule favors voluntary action by business over government-mandated action. Where voluntary action is judged not to be feasible for cost or other reasons and where analysis of social needs and expectations indicates a substantial probability of governmental action, the strategy favors constructive participation by business in designing the prospective regulation. The strategic objective is to demonstrate the concern of business for the public interest by contributing to the development of solutions to serious social problems.

There is a simple rationale for business commitment to this strategic objective. While the modern industrialized economy has made enormous contributions to the physical well-being of its host society, it has also created wounding side effects—physical, social, and psychic. The advance of living standards for most people to a state of comfort, if not of luxury, has stimulated interest in the quality of life. The business community in general and the leaders of major corporations in particular have been seen as generally insensitive or indifferent to the side effects of industrialization. Often, they have opposed efforts to ameliorate what many observers judged to be serious social problems. They have permitted the business interest to be identified as different from, even opposed to, the general social interest as well as to the specific interests of significant and politically powerful social groups.

The central problem is not popular hostility to or ignorance about the business system. Rather, it is discontent with some aspects of the system's behavior and, more broadly, with some effects of advanced industrialization in an affluent society. When business is seen as fully concerned about societal expectations and about ameliorating or removing the wounding side effects, corporations and their leaders will experience a rising trend of public respect and trust.

The third dimension of the matrix is, of course, time. The evolving social climate for business must be tracked far enough in advance of the development of strong pressures for specific changes in corporate behavior to allow time for consideration of voluntary initiatives. Most companies have a poor record for anticipating important public pressures for changed social performance. Strong demands for legislation and regulation in the areas of fair employment, environmental pollution, consumer protection, and safety and hygiene of the workplace have surprised business leaders repeatedly. This failure of vision has forced corporations into a reactive posture and has limited their flexibility for response. It has contributed to the general perception of business as an adversary of the public interest. It has also severely constrained the ability of the business community to influence the development of public attitudes and the design of remedial legislation.

SENIOR MANAGEMENT PARTICIPATION IN SOCIAL
AND ECONOMIC PERFORMANCE DECISIONS

In formulating policies and programs for social and economic performance the chief executive officer will find it helpful to draw on all elements of his senior management structure for information and counsel. As senior executives share a common understanding of the compelling reasons for the commitment, and as they contribute to the design effort, their sense of responsibility for translating the commitment into reality will be strengthened. This attitude will be transmitted, in turn, to middle managers who make the system work day by day.

The chief executive's first resource should be his board of directors. Strengthened by outside directors whose combined experience and knowledge encompass business, government, and a variety of other interests, the board can counsel and support the chief executive in several valuable ways. This assistance will be most effectively focused if a board committee is created with special responsibility for thinking through social performance in relation to environmental opportunities and challenges and also to the effectiveness and efficiency of internal resource utilization. The board can pose discerning questions about proposed corporate social performance initiatives and equally about failures to act in circumstances that seem to require or favor action. It can sustain the chief executive's confidence in the correctness of his chosen course when he encounters disaffection from operating associates or from the leaders of other business organizations. Its official endorsement of his comprehensive social and economic performance strategy will also help, if necessary, to rebut any criticism that may arise from shareholders.

The Role of Middle Management

The environment within which middle managers work differs from the senior management environment in a number of important ways. Middle managers have a direct exposure to operating problems in factory, marketplace, and office from which top managers are usually shielded except at times of crisis. The decisions that determine middle managers' short-term income and status and their long-term career prospects are based on different performance criteria than those applicable to senior managers. Middle managers see the organizational structure within which they function from a different viewpoint, which determines how they assess the organization's authority hierarchy and its politics. They are at a different stage in their life cycles than their seniors, with different family responsibilities and different relationships with their communities. In effect, the entire complex of experiences to which they are exposed, on and off the job, is different from the experience matrix of top management.

DOMINANT ATTITUDES OF MIDDLE MANAGERS

Middle managers can be described as strongly career-oriented, attuned to economic rather than social performance, highly sensitive to formal short-term performance measurements, focused on self more than on organization, and disposed to view managerial career progression as influenced by job performance and organizational politics. Such attitudes affect how they appraise the concept of corporate social performance, how they perceive and evaluate statements of corporate policy, and how they respond to social performance programs that impinge (or are perceived to impinge) on their duties and responsibilities. This is a critical relationship. With the exception of a few middle managers who, for reasons of nature or nurture, may be particularly sensitive to social issues, the typical frame of reference for decision is the perceived career effect of any corporate social performance policy or program.

Those in corporate leadership positions who want to introduce social performance objectives as a coordinate of economic performance objectives must thoroughly understand this motivational issue. Senior officers of a number of companies have faced the same issue when they introduced a formal long-range planning procedure. Middle managers perceived the reward/penalty system as closely tied to short-run operating results measured by the annual profit/sales/cost/return-on-assets budget. Beneath managers' superficial compliance with the numerical formalities of the long-range planning exercises, primary attention continued to be directed to maximizing short-run results. Managers resisted making investments or incurring costs aimed at strengthening the base for long-term performance if they believed such commitments would significantly depress short-term operating results. They did this even while acknowledging privately their awareness that their decisions would probably create future problems. In their judgment, the signals emanating from the perceived reward/penalty system reported the real interest of top management more accurately than did those suggested by the newly-introduced planning procedure.

DETERMINING INFLUENCES FOR MIDDLE MANAGERS' BEHAVIOR

A middle manager's behavior is largely determined by his assessment of the factors he perceives as most influential in promoting his career. Research and operating experience indicate that five factors, present in every manager's organizational environment, override all other considerations. They are highly visible to the manager, for himself and also for his peers. They are the center of attention when managers appraise their prospects, alone or in the company of their associates.

The first is the manager's job description: the formal definition of the responsibilities and duties of the position he occupies, his line of reporting to the next higher organizational level, his authority span over lower levels, and his coordinating relationships across organizational boundaries. This charter serves as the primary blueprint for his general field of action. However, since it is usually drafted in the most comprehensive language and rarely indicates the relative importance of the several elements of the job assignment, the manager must look elsewhere for necessary guidance on what to emphasize and how to implement his top priorities.

The second factor is the manager's perception of the specific performance standards used by his superiors in evaluating him. In almost all organizations these criteria are expressed in the unit budget. It matters little (in effect on behavior, not necessarily in effect on attitude and morale) whether a manager participates in formulating his unit's budget or has it imposed by higher authority. In either case, the officially approved budget is the visible benchmark. It becomes the performance commitment. It determines priorities of management attention and action. In some organizations, the operating budget may be supplemented by certain nonoperating commitments of a formal written character covering such areas as recruiting, training, and development of subordinates. When present, these goals command attention, although usually of subsidiary importance to operating objectives. If operating or time pressures squeeze a manager, activities related to the secondary goals tend to be curtailed.

Even explicit operating budget objectives require additional refinement and reinforcement as a guide to a manager's behavior. Most budgets contain possibilities for trade-offs: more of one element can be secured by accepting less of another. This needed refinement and reinforcement is provided by the third factor—the formal performance assessment system that defines the budget items for which performance is specifically measured and the time frame to which measurement is applied. This information may be adequately communicated to a manager by periodic reports comparing results obtained with budget objectives. If the budget and periodic measurement of performance are laid out in complex detail, however, a manager asks especially which items regularly arouse his superiors' greatest interest—the items for which above or below-budget performance regularly generates praise or criticsm.

The fourth factor is the manager's perception of the organization's reward/penalty system, as officially described and as he observes its application to himself and his peers. If the official description is at variance with the observed pattern of actions, it is, of course, the latter that is believed. The intervening gap is ascribed to the working of the organization's political system which then, as the fifth factor, becomes the object of particularly intense analysis directed at developing a degree of understanding that will permit the manager to operate successfully within the system and even to manipulate it to his own advantage.

As practically all business organizations have functioned for many years, these five principal influences have directed managers' interest and effort toward economic objectives. This concentration on economic performance, not only above social considerations, but even, as a number of recently reported instances have revealed, above normal ethical considerations is reinforced for most managers by almost every significant conditioning factor in their training and experience.

An important conditioning element for managers within the referent culture was, of course, their educational experience. For a large proportion of today's middle managers this experience has included a business curriculum at either college or M.B.A. level. Issues related to corporate social performance have had only minimal representation in most business school curricula, and the primacy of economic objectives in all policy formulation and performance evaluation situations is rarely subjected to analytical discussion. The same relative emphasis is reflected in the content of most executive development programs, whether conducted by graduate business schools, trade and professional organizations, or within corporations.

An even more pervasive, if subtler, influence on middle managers is their perception of society's prevailing standards for measuring personal accomplishment. Although clearly there is a rising disposition among millions of adults to question corporate social behavior, the governing philosophy in our culture is still overwhelmingly materialistic. "Getting ahead" is still generally measured by acquisition of money and goods. As a people we are just beginning to confront some of the hard trade-offs among economic and social objectives—for example, as between ample energy supplies and an expanding economy, on one side, and some of the more extreme scenarios of dedicated environmentalists, on the other. It is at least interesting—and possibly of substantial significance—that the initial popular reaction in a number of tough trade-off situations has been to back away from extreme standards of environmental hygiene when confronted by a high price in terms of curtailed economic growth.

Middle managers are not sheltered from the doubts and questions that are troubling a growing number outside corporate management ranks. But they are under more pressure, subject to stronger motivation, than outsiders to resist any intellectual or emotional accommodation that might appear to superiors or peers to be a weakening of commitment to traditional objectives.

The principal criticisms of corporate social performance naturally have been directed to top management. Middle managers are often confronted by specific local issues—protests by women and minorities over employment and promotion practices, protests by community groups over environmental pollution incidents, probing by communications media into the effects of production cutbacks or plant closings, union protest over issues of safety and hygiene of working conditions. Yet in the absence of established corporate policies, these issues are transmitted rapidly to higher authority for guidance or resolution. Because of such referrals, middle managers rarely experience the intellectual exercise of carefully exploring social benefits and costs—a valuable aid in becoming mentally and emotionally comfortable with a new fundamental concept in corporate governance.

From the middle managers' viewpoint, corporate social performance policy statements and program decisions usually appear with little advance warning or educational preparation. Suddenly managers are confronted by new performance requirements that not only revise established standards and practices but also threaten to constrain their ability to achieve the established operating goals which they view as their primary responsibility.

An instruction to take positive steps to hire women and minorities and to promote those already employed is more than a simple modification in personnel procedures. It raises difficult problems of reactions by existing employees, effects on seniority practices, threats to productivity, and customer attitudes. An instruction to revise procurement practices with the objective of directing more business to minority-owned suppliers is more than a modest revision in the placement of purchase orders. It poses troubling considerations about acquisition costs, quality assurance, delivery schedules, continuity of operations, and even the need to provide special management counsel and financial assistance to marginal suppliers. An instruction to include investment for pollution control in capital budget proposals is more than a procedural stipulation. It raises the probability of reduced return on assets and curtailed appropriations for the support of ongoing or new productive activities. These are not trivial issues for middle managers. They are loaded with economic performance and career implications that cannot fail to be troubling and confusing. These disturbing effects are likely to be reinforced if, as is usually the case, the social performance policies and operating directives are communicated downstream as individual top management decisions, rather than in the context of a comprehensive reorientation of the total business aimed at coordinating economic and social performance.

Against this background, it should not be surprising that middle managers are commonly skeptical, indifferent, or hostile toward social performance policies and programs communicated from corporate headquarters. At one end of the spectrum, managers assess the announcements as designed for external publics, without significant meaning within the organization. At the other extreme, they see a threat to their own careers. Skepticism leads to inaction and, at best, to superficial gestures toward compliance in anticipation of weak follow-up through supervisory channels. Fear leads to hostility and a disposition to identify and magnify difficulties in putting instructions into effect.

Another issue may be of even greater substance than the negative attitudes. Some social performance policies and programs call for knowledge and skills that many middle managers lack and know they lack, or expose managers to problems they prefer not to face because they are uncertain about their competence for handling them successfully. A manager who has never supervised an employee group in which blacks or Latins constitute a significant element may well wonder whether he will confront problems of communication, motivation, discipline, and productivity. He may anticipate a degree of culture shock to which he will not readily adjust. Regardless of his assessment of his own ability to administer effectively in such a situation, he may have serious concern about difficult frictional relationships within his subordinate group, particularly if some members of the established group sense the possibility of reverse discrimination.

Culture shock of a different character is likely to be anticipated by middle managers who have no experience in working with women in subordinated or peer positions. At the least, they sense the introduction of new and uncomfortable relationships and disturbance of familiar behavior patterns. Middle managers who have never represented their companies in confrontations with community or interest group leaders, or with the media, have good reason to doubt their competence in such situations. There is little in their earlier training and work experience on which they can draw for guidance.

The superficially attractive solution to all of these difficulties of attitude, knowledge, and skill is to educate managers to understand and handle their new duties and responsibilities. Carefully planned educational programs, designed with a grasp of managers' genuine concerns as well as their cultural blocks, will help, particularly in adding to their understanding of social changes and their perception of operating problems in carrying out specific social performance programs. But education alone is not likely to have any material effect in converting negative into positive attitudes. Indifferent or destructive attitudes reflect a conflict between managers' perception of the requirements for effective implementation of social performance policies and programs and their perception of the requirements for advancing their own careers. Until this perceived conflict is removed, any educational effort will be handicapped by the absence of strong motivation among participating managers and of clear reinforcement through the formal reward/penalty system. As every professional educator knows, strong motivation to learn and clear reinforcement of lessons learned, through consistent rewards and penalties, are essential for successful learning and for constructive behavior.

With respect to the educational program itself, it should also be observed that the introduction of social performance considerations into business organizations is a genuine innovation. Developing the required managerial knowledge and skills will generate a need for new educational materials. No more than a beginning has been made toward defining either the information requirements or the analytical techniques to forecast trends in public expectations and demands for corporate social performance. Little is known about how to relate projected trends to the task of defining practical opportunities for and limitations on responses by individual companies. New accounting concepts and systems must be developed to facilitate the extension of cost/benefit analysis to comprehend social as well as economic considerations. In short, progress in identifying and providing needed materials for the educational experience must be supported by appropriate motivational and operating machinery.

Redesigning the Total Internal Governance System

What is required is comprehensive redesign of the total internal governance system to reflect the incorporation of new social objectives along with traditional economic objectives. The existing structure was designed to facilitate and motivate the accomplishment of economic goals. Until this structure is appropriately modified, policy pronouncements and program determinations at the senior administrative level will not be fully credible at lower organizational levels. Where attainment of social performance goals is perceived as interfering with the attainment of economic performance goals, the former will be sacrificed to the latter to the extent necessary to assure satisfactory economic performance. In these circumstances, skepticism about senior management's sincerity will fester and educational programs will not be effective.

The next step in adapting the corporate management system to put social objectives on a par with economic objectives is clear communication by the chief executive officer of the meaning of the new corporate philosophy and the rationale for adopting it. The statement should note that what is projected is not an erosion of the organization's economic mission. Rather, it is an accommodation to the facts of life in contemporary society, an accommodation that will be mandated by the society if voluntary initiatives are not taken by business. The communication should point out that in many areas of social concern with business behavior there are opportunities for corporate actions that will be economically advantageous to organizations whose managers have the imagination and will to act vigorously ahead of competitors. In other areas where action by a single company may not be feasible for competitive reasons, advantageous opportunities may still be discovered to influence the standards and procedures of public regulation.

This is not a simple message for the chief executive officer to articulate or for middle managers to understand and accept. Understanding and acceptance can be encouraged and assisted by a variety of supporting measures. The unqualified endorsement of the new administrative philosophy by the board of directors must be visible to all managers. This endorsement will be strengthened if the com-

position, structure, and work of the board reflects a commitment
to broader participation in membership by qualified persons who
are knowledgeable about societal concerns and who will closely
scrutinize management performance in these areas. Understanding
and acceptance can be further assisted by small group meetings in
which senior line and staff officers take the lead in discussing the
rationale for the changed view of the mission of the business and
articulating their unqualified commitment to it.

This top-down communications process is no more than a stage
set, however. Most middle managers will not accept social performance as a concept with real operating significance until they see
it incorporated in specific terms in their assigned duties and
responsibilities, until specific time-phased social performance
objectives are built into their operating budgets, until their accomplishment of these objectives is systematically measured just as their
accomplishment of budgeted economic targets is measured, and
until each manager's measured social performance is visibly brought
within the scope of the reward/penalty system. What all this involves is no less than a major transformation in corporate governance.

This transformation will be both easier and more difficult to
accomplish than was the initial institution of the administrative
system that defines economic performance objectives for operating
units, determines responsibility for achieving them, measures results, and motivates managerial behavior. It will be easier because
it utilizes existing performance concepts and existing control systems. It will be more difficult because the initial steps to define
specific social performance objectives will immediately reveal the
complex network of relationships among economic and social performance objectives, their competitive claims on limited corporate
resources, and the need to develop a vocabulary and an arithmetic
appropriate for describing and evaluating economic and social costs
and benefits within an integrated decision system. As in the experience with economic performance control systems, the specifica-
tion of objectives and related resource requirements will promptly
illuminate conflicting claims and compel managers to determine
priorities. These judgments then will have to be worked through
trade-offs among social performance programs and also through
trade-offs between economic and social objectives.

In spite of these difficulties, there should be no doubt that middle managers' understanding, acceptance, and implementation of social performance policies and programs—whatever their content as determined by senior management—are dependent on full and specific incorporation of the policies and programs within the administrative system of the business. Anything short of such a comprehensive approach will weaken the credibility of the corporate posture among the managers whose commitment is essential for converting policy into practice.

SPECIAL MANAGEMENT TRAINING NEEDS

Some of the administrative tasks associated with social performance programs raise problems that are outside the education and experience of most managers. Dealing with these issues calls for skills that few operating executives have developed through prior training and practice or can work up on their own initiative. They need training, just as do operating managers in corporations that install formal long-range planning systems.

The most urgent training needs are in two areas. The first is managing nondiscriminatory personnel policies and practices in factory, office, and management ranks. The second is managing relationships with external publics and with communications media. In both areas, the critical issue is not what to do, but how to do it. What to do is easily defined. The difficulty here, as noted above, is credibility, and the tactics that will strengthen credibility are readily applied by determined, sophisticated senior management. How to do it is another matter altogether, one in which imaginative training programs in a few companies are already making valuable contributions.

In personnel administration, the central problem can be described as one of cultural adjustment, although the term should not be interpreted as dismissing substantive issues in such sensitive areas as seniority prerogatives and perceived reverse discrimination. Friction and resistance in these areas are not trivial matters, of course, but external social pressures, as well as governmental actions, are working to assist corporate managers to develop formulas of accommodation that will be acceptable to conflicting interests. On the whole, there is more noise than substance here, and even the noise will diminish in an expanding economy.

The cultural adjustment is less spectacular but more difficult to handle. Most middle managers are not at ease with an organizational environment in which many management positions are occupied by women and members of minority groups. The problem is not significantly different from that met by American managers who are posted to a foreign country where their associates are nationals, and who are not adequately prepared in language, customs, traditions, attitudes—all that goes to make up a unique culture.

As experience in multinationals suggests, left to their own resources most managers ultimately learn how to make the essential cultural adjustments, although often painfully and slowly. Some cannot come to terms with the alien environment and have to be withdrawn. Carefully planned training programs can build the understanding and develop the skills required for a faster and easier adjustment. As a useful side effect, such programs may also facilitate early identification of those who cannot be helped to function effectively outside their native culture.

Training needs are both more obvious and considerably simpler in the area of relationships with external publics and communications media. For most middle managers this is a radical enlargement of traditional job responsibilities. They have little preparation in training or experience for dealing with community or special interest groups in adversary situations; such as those connected with environmental contamination, factory hygiene, and personnel practices. With rare exceptions, they have had no exposure to media representatives in potentially hostile circumstances, no occasion to formulate policy positions under pressure and articulate them clearly and forcefully to reporters and before television cameras. Yet with growing frequency, middle managers responsible for plant, geographic, or product operations find themselves in positions where they must speak for their organizations and where what they say and how they say it can have a critical effect, positive or negative, on public attitudes and even on governmental decisions.

They need help, and, fortunately, they know they need help. So, for that matter, do senior corporate officers who are also frequently called upon to speak for their organizations in adversary face-to-face situations and on television. A well-designed training program can build the kind of understanding of constituency group attitudes and tactics and of the politics of media relations that is essential for developing reasonable and constructive corporate positions that effectively accommodate public and corporate interests. It can also improve managers' communications skills and strengthen their confidence in their ability to address public audiences face-to-face and through print and electronic media. As a not inconsequential by-product, it can also bring to the attention of senior officers individuals who are unusually effective in such situations, an ability that is likely to be given increasing attention in future promotion decisions.

Index

Accountability, 40
  strategy of, 139-52
Accounting, 21-22, 111-38
  Commission on Auditors' Responsibilities, 132-37
  control of, 114-20
  as control device, 113-14
  development of, 113
  formulation of standards, 116, 120-24
  oil and gas industry and, 115-20
  questionable payments, 124-32, 134-35
  Securities and Exchange Commission and, 116, 120-24, 131
Accounting Principles Board, 123, 133
  Opinion No. 2, 123
  Opinion No. 4, 123
Ackerman, Robert, 85
Advertising, deceptive, 23
Advisory Committee on Corporate Disclosure, 77
Affirmative action programs, 161
Airlines, 22
American Bar Association, 24
American Express Company, 71-72
American Institute of Certified Public Accountants (AICPA), 24, 116, 128, 131, 133
American Telephone and Telegraph, 139, 144, 149
Angola, 52, 53
Annual meeting, 151
Anshen, Melvin, 5, 153-75
Antitrust action, 9, 16
Apartheid, 39
ATO, 39
Auditing (see Accounting)
Automobile companies, 15, 17, 20, 33

Barnard, Chester, 10
Becton Dickinson and Company, 45
Berle, A. A., 15

Bethlehem Steel Corporation, 73
Better Business Bureaus, 23
Bishop, Joseph, Jr., 71
Board of directors (see Directors)
Boulding, Kenneth, 61, 74
Brandeis, Louis D., 58
Bribes, 5, 23, 39, 126-28
Bullock Report, 48
Business Roundtable, The, 24, 68, 84, 97, 103-4, 108-9

Campaign contributions, 23, 39
Campaign GM, 51-52
Capitalism, 11-13
Cary, William, 72
Chartering, 3, 35, 41, 50
Chatov, Robert, 121
Chief executive officer (CEO), 91, 99, 100, 104-6, 150-52, 154-55, 157-59, 163-64
Chrysler Corporation, 39
Clark, John Maurice, 8, 24, 36-37
Class action suits, 27
Coalition Against the SST, 92
Codetermination (*Mitbestimmung*), 46-49
Cohen, Manuel, 132
Commission on Auditors' Responsibilities, 97, 132-37
Committee on Corporate Laws of the American Bar Association, 97, 108-9
Competition, 11, 60, 109
Computers, 146
Conference Board, 24
Consolidated Edison, 20
Consumer protection, 3, 17, 23, 50-51, 60, 161, 163
Control (see Accounting)
Control Data Corporation, 15
Corporate Director's Guidebook, 108-9

The American Assembly

About The American Assembly

The American Assembly was established by Dwight D. Eisenhower at Columbia University in 1950. It holds nonpartisan meetings and publishes authoritative books to illuminate issues of United States policy.

An affiliate of Columbia, with offices in the Graduate School of Business, the Assembly is a national educational institution incorporated in the State of New York.

The Assembly seeks to provide information, stimulate discussion, and evoke independent conclusions in matters of vital public interest.

AMERICAN ASSEMBLY SESSIONS

At least two national programs are initiated each year. Authorities are retained to write background papers presenting essential data and defining the main issues in each subject.

A group of men and women representing a broad range of experience, competence, and American leadership meet for several days to discuss the Assembly topic and consider alternatives for national policy.

All Assemblies follow the same procedure. The background papers are sent to participants in advance of the Assembly. The Assembly meets in small groups for four or five lengthy periods. All groups use the same agenda. At the close of these informal sessions, participants adopt in plenary sessions a final report of findings and recommendations.

Regional, state, and local Assemblies are held following the national session at Arden House. Assemblies have also been held in England, Switzerland, Malaysia, Canada, the Caribbean, South America, Central America, the Philippines, and Japan. Over one hundred thirty institutions have co-sponsored one or more Assemblies.

ARDEN HOUSE

Home of the American Assembly and scene of the national sessions is Arden House, which was given to Columbia University in 1950 by W. Averell Harriman. E. Roland Harriman joined his brother in contributing toward adaptation of the property for conference purposes. The buildings and surrounding land, known as the Harriman Campus of Columbia University, are 50 miles north of New York City.

Arden House is a distinguished conference center. It is self-supporting and operates throughout the year for use by organizations with educational objectives.

The background papers for each Assembly are published in cloth and paperbound editions for use by individuals, libraries, businesses, public agencies, nongovernmental organizations, educational institutions, discussion and service groups. In this way the deliberations of Assembly sessions are continued and extended.

The subject of Assembly programs to date are:

1951——United States-Western Europe Relationships
1952——Inflation
1953——Economic Security for Americans
1954——The United States' Stake in the United Nations
——The Federal Government Service
1955——United States Agriculture
——The Forty-Eight States
1956——The Representation of the United States Abroad
——The United States and the Far East
1957——International Stability and Progress
——Atoms for Power
1958——The United States and Africa
——United States Monetary Policy
1959——Wages, Prices, Profits, and Productivity
——The United States and Latin America
1960——The Federal Government and Higher Education
——The Secretary of State
——Goals for Americans
1961——Arms Control: Issues for the Public
——Outer Space: Prospects for Man and Society
1962——Automation and Technological Change
——Cultural Affairs and Foreign Relations
1963——The Population Dilemma
——The United States and the Middle East
1964——The United States and Canada
——The Congress and America's Future
1965——The Courts, the Public, and the Law Explosion
——The United States and Japan
1966——State Legislatures in American Politics
——A World of Nuclear Powers?
——The United States and the Philippines
——Challenges to Collective Bargaining

FT. MYERS